SAILORMAN

D1590170

Captain Navvy Brooks, the Author and 'passengers'

SAILORMAN

A BARGE-MASTER'S STORY
by Captain Jim Uglow MBE

**Photographs
Collected by Tony Farnham**

CONWAY MARITIME PRESS
GREENWICH

Published by
Conway Maritime Press Limited
7 Nelson road, Greenwich, London SE10
ISBN 085177 085 1

Cover photography by
Ambrose Greenway
Design by
Jon Blackmore Design, London
Phototypesetting and Printing by
Royden Greene Ltd., Derby
Binding by
Backhurst & Taylor, Nottingham.

I dedicate this book to all bargemen,
past and present.

Foreword

This is a true life story and consists of experiences that actually happened. I have not had to conjure up, with the aid of a vivid imagination and a few half truths, a story to make plausible reading. The original manuscript was written on night watches during the war, when, manned by a crew of inexperienced lads, I had to be prepared to dash on deck at a moments notice, so I used my writing as a method of keeping awake. I had to rely entirely upon my memory for dates and names. Critics will probably find that there are inaccuracies with regard to dates but otherwise it is authentic. It is mostly about barges and bargemen, but is in the main a personal narrative.

In 1947 I had four copies of the manuscript typed out. Two copies I gave to friends and the other two were entrusted to somebody with a view to publishing and finally disappeared. It was only in 1970 when moving into my present house, my original scrawls were found in an old cardboard box. A few months ago Tony Farnham, in his enthusiasm for the subject, volunteered to sort it out and get it typed. He and his wife Eileen deserve all credit for their efforts in once more producing it in readable form. To bring the book up to date I have incorporated two more war incidents and a chapter on post-war barge racing.

Most of the people mentioned in my original manuscript are now dead, although there are still a few old Skippers alive, including Jimmy Mole and old 'Dick the Dagger' still lively at the age of a hundred. Obviously many characters should be referred to in the past tense. It is curious, with regard to the chapter suggesting that coasting should be kept for the purpose of training young lads in seamanship, that we now have the two fine auxiliary schooners *Sir Winston Churchill* and *Malcolm Miller* fulfilling this purpose.

In conclusion I will just say that due to the speed of modern conditions, barges for several years have not been a commercial proposition as freight carriers, the exceptions being the few that are let out on charter for pleasure and business. Apart from these, the only survivors have been converted to power or are houseboats and those sailed entirely for sport and pleasure. If it was not for enthusiasts like Tony Farnham and others like him who do a tremendous amount of work in the cause of fostering interest in these craft, they would soon be as extinct as the Dodo.

GREENHITHE, 1974

Contents

Acknowledgements

**The publishers would like to thank
the following for their help
with photographic research:**

Mr C Alston; Mr L Arnold; Mr H Batch
the Brooks family, May, Charles and Lawrence
Conway Picture Library; Mrs M Creasy; Miss E Everard
Capt J Farthing; Mrs V Hart; Mr W Josh; Capt H Miller
Capt J Mole; Capt J Nunn; Mr G Osbon
Mr C R Temple; The Thames Barge Sailing Club
and especially Tony and Eileen Farnham

Plates

Introduction

The era of sail has practically passed. The clippers and ocean going tramps under canvas were the first to give way to the speedier conditions demanded in this modern age; after them the barquentines and brigs employed in the coal trade disappeared; then the West Country schooners and ketches until now the only craft still employed commercially under sail, in rapidly diminishing numbers, is the Thames barge. I, and many others who have served our time in sail, think that this is detrimental to Britain as a sea power. Whilst appreciating that sail as a commercial proposition is practically finished, we, from our personal experience, know that the modern seaman falls far short of the standard demanded twenty and thirty years ago. I have no doubt that the material is there, but the youngsters going to sea today have not been taught in a correct manner. Also the improved conditions now granted to seamen tend to soften them. They—and I speak of the majority—have not that old fashioned pride in their ship and boast that their ship is the Sailing Ship . . . . . which has a name for being smart either in sailing or appearance, or both. The main concern is how many hours overtime they can claim and they look forward to finding a ship that will discharge close to their front door once a week. Sail taught one pride of ship, initiative, comradeship, discipline and smartness.

Every old sailorman knew that if the Master of the vessel was smart, he could put a ship under full canvas alongside a dock head or wharf for a matter of seconds. If the crew were equally smart (and they were taught to be) one of them would jump ashore and take a quick turn on a rope to hold the vessel in position. Both Master and crew knew this manoeuvre had got to be executed promptly. If the crew failed to take a risk by jumping or were not quick enough in some other respect, it meant that the vessel would fall away, the anchor would have to be let go and later hove up on a hand windlass. Furthermore after letting go the anchor and bringing the vessel up, the sails had to be furled, a boat manned and possibly sixty fathoms of three inch line sculled or rowed away to the pier head. This having been made fast, the weight had to be taken on a hand winch, the anchor hove up and the vessel slowly and laboriously hove back alongside.

At the present day with diesel engines, a Master can still put his ship alongside in the same competent way as the old times. There is always the chance that if there is a strong offshore wind, the craft will blow away from the quay if the crew are not smart—but the consequences do not demand the physical labour formerly required by the crew. Many a time in recent years I have seen a modern motor coaster put alongside in a proper manner and while the Mate or one of the crew were expostulating that there was nobody ashore to take the ropes, the ship has blown away from the quay. With a few choice remarks from the Master and judicious use of the engine room telegraph, the ship has again been manoeuvred into position and somebody has plucked up sufficient courage to step on to the shore and take a rope.

Under canvas the crew took pride in their spars and gear and used to vie with each other to see who could properly scrape, oil and varnish a spar in less time than the other. Rigging was black varnished and all chafing gear properly finished off and trim. With the advent of steel spars and buff paint another of the finer points of sailoring was lost.

I think it is primarally a Government responsibility but the major shipping lines could assist in devising some scheme whereby every person joining the present Merchant Navy, should spend twelve months under sail. Temporarily the few barges that are left under sail could be provided with accommodation—accommodation in the old sense—for ten apprentices. With an experienced Master the vessels could be employed commercially and the losses be borne by the Government. I also think that if ten 300 ton sea-going sailing barges were built, even today, with enough accommodation for ten lads, they could be run with only a small financial loss and would teach 1000 youngsters a year far more in the way of seamanship than they would get in three years of sea school or even three years practical experience in power vessels.

One thing that has been lost never to return is the sense of achievement felt by Masters and crew under sail. Possibly in company with other vessels on a passage, by trimming a sail or easing a sheet, they would have the pleasure of seeing their vessel drawing away from her rivals. Many a time, in friendly rivalry with other Masters, bound for the same destination, I have sailed for a new hat. This meant that the Master of the first vessel to arrive was given the price of a hat by his rival or rivals. From the point of view of crews, having been taught how to ride and furl a topsail in a gale of wind, whilst possibly not caring for the order when given, they still had the satisfactory feeling of having accomplished a difficult job when they once more stepped down on to the deck.

The Creed of the Coasting & Home Trade Shipowners. (Usual Saturday Sailing Co. Ltd.)

Oh, day of rest and gladness
Oh, Sailorman's delight
To stay in port of sadness
Would surely not be right
So Saturday doth see him
Each mooring line set free
And leave to spend each Sunday
Upon the glorious sea.

From Saturday to Monday
The Office Staff must stay
At home and spend each Sunday
In some unfruitful way
But we upon God's ocean
No carking cares shall know
Our work is our devotion
As o'er the sea we go.

The Pubs are closed on Sunday
Because they cannot trust
The weak and wayward shoreman
From going on the bust
But we whose hearts are cleansed
From sordid thoughts of beer
With joy that never endeth
Shall serve the Lord out here.

Please God the gentle sailor
Will never know the pain
The Managers must suffer
When their attempts are vain
To clear the ships each week-end
And get them off to sea
For ships tied up on Sunday
Would spoil Eternity.

CHAPTER 1

Running away to sea

I have always been proud of the fact that I am descended from a sea-going family. My father served thirty years in the Royal Navy, attaining the rank of Lieutenant Shipwright. My grandfather also served a lifetime in the Navy as a blacksmith, without distinction as far as I know, but I still have his medal for service in the Crimean War. My great-grandfather was reputed to have sailed his own ketch from the port of Plymouth, and his father also went to sea.

When I was ten years of age, my father decided that as soon as I was old enough I would be apprenticed to the Merchant service. Even at that early stage, for some unknown reason, he picked on the firm of Elders and Fyffe as my future employers.

At this time our household consisted of my parents, two stepbrothers, by a former marriage of my mother, both older than myself, and my young sister and brother. My greatest treat in those days was when my father took me to dine in the wardroom of various ships in which he served. First the old *Albermarle,* then in succession the *Crecy, Shannon* and *Cornwallis.* I also remember being balanced on the knees of various Japanese officers when a ship of the Imperial Japanese Navy was on a goodwill visit—the *Ancona* if my memory serves me right. This was about 1910. In 1915, the *Cornwallis* proceeded to the Dardanelles, my father serving as chief carpenter. He survived the sinking of this ship, when she was torpedoed off Malta after the evacuation of Gallipoli. My elder stepbrother was by then in the Army and my other stepbrother living in a hostel and munition-making at Woolwich. My mother, like many women before her, was indulging in a life of gaiety and

15

extravagance and in consequence we remaining three children were neglected and left largely to our own devices.

After the sinking of the *Cornwallis*, the crew returned to England to be recommissioned. When my father came home after two years at sea, he found a three months old baby in a pram, a pile of debts and three very neglected children. After a succession of violent scenes my mother left with her paramour and the baby and just disappeared from our lives. I was then eleven years of age. Dad installed a housekeeper and tried to make a real home for us but his heart was not in it and he proceeded to drink himself to death. After a period in Chatham Barracks he was commissioned in the old battleship *Prince George* which had two funnels abreast. She was moored in the Salt Pan Reach in the Medway, and the old chap got a fair amount of time at home. He obtained a fourteen foot ship's boat with a mast and spritsail in which we had good fun. He taught me to sail her and later when he was transferred to the cruiser *Gibraltar* I was left in sole charge of my first craft at the age of twelve. Our first housekeeper was a motherly soul and looked after us well for eighteen months before she emigrated to Australia. Then followed four others in quick succession who pawned most of the household goods while Dad was away. In all this domestic upheaval I managed to obtain a scholarship to a secondary school and I was still to be apprenticed.

While sailing my boat up and down the Medway I had naturally seen many sailing barges, the Associated Portland Cement Manufacturers (APCM) running a fleet of these craft from the various cement mills between Chatham and Maidstone to the London Docks with cement for export, but had then no interest in them. In 1919 I made friends with a lad called Alf Beard whose mother gave me an occasional square meal. At the time I rather looked down on him because his father was Skipper of a barge, the S/B *Sportsman* I believe. Later in the year my interest in these craft quickened when Alf told me that during the summer holidays he had been to France on his dad's barge. In my ignorance I told him that he was lying and that barges only went as far as Southend and London. He then informed me that the craft had loaded a cargo of pitch from Beckton to Calais and that many barges went to all northern ports of France. By this time I was running wild, often playing truant from school to go sailing by myself.

16

Running away to sea

In October of 1919 I decided to sail to Sheerness. The boat was moored just below Gillingham pier and I got an old boatman, Don Kier by name, to put me off in his boat to the moorings. This old chap had told me many an interesting yarn of days in real sailing ships, and on this particular day warned me that there was a SW gale and it was not safe for me to sail. Even in those days I was very hot-headed and would not listen to good advice. I managed to set the mainsail and cast off the moorings and away I went. As I jybed in the various reaches the boat shipped a considerable amount of water, but having neither sense nor fear I was perfectly happy and managed to steer and bale so as to keep her reasonably free from water. After passing Port Victoria I got a bit of a lee and tried to lower the mainsail with the intention of sticking her ashore for the night. Unfortunately the halliards had slipped off the sheave at the mast head and jammed so that I could not lower the sail. I had not the sense to bring her into the wind with a slack sheet so kept running. After passing Garrison Point I had no idea where I was going or what to expect, but found I was rapidly overhauling a barge under foresail and mainsail who had already pinned his sheet and vang preparatory to hauling up for Yantlet. I had sense enough to sail to leeward of him while his huge mainsail sucked the wind out of my sail. I shouted an explanation of my difficulties and the Skipper told me to come alongside. I did so and the Mate of the barge promptly solved the problem of the jammed halliards by breaking the mast off short at the thwart. I was wet, cold and hungry but the only sympathy I got was a lecture on my foolhardiness. There were several barges anchored off Yantlet and the Skipper of the barge said he could not stop because he had to catch a ship in London. I cannot remember her name but she belonged to the BPCM and had black sails. He pointed out a barge which he said was bound to Rochester and would tow me back next day. He explained that he was going to sail ahead and to windward of her and then cast me adrift to drop back to the other barge. I managed to do this and made fast the painter to a cleat on the taffrail. It was now dark and nobody came on deck to enquire what was happening. I made fast, baled the boat out, and then wrapped myself in the wet sail and went to sleep on the floorboards. I was awake before dawn, still wet and miserable.
Shortly after daybreak a man's head popped up from the

SAILORMAN

cabin hatchway and had a look round. His look of amazement ended with the query, "What are you doing here Sonny?" I explained, and he said, "Come on board you poor little B." I followed him down the cabin where his wife — who was acting as Mate — was frying sausages over a big open fire. The Skipper said, "Look what I've found Lil. Put some more sausages in the pan and give him a mug of hot tea." 'Good souls' — I was only thirteen years old and nearer to tears in that warm cabin than I had been in an open boat for twenty hours without food. The Skipper told me that he had kept anchored during the last flood tide because it was blowing so hard and he did not want to tack up the Medway in the dark with only his wife to help him. He explained that after we had breakfast he would heave up the anchor now that it was finer, save the last of the ebb tide down through the swatchway and take the flood up the Medway. They dried my clothes, the woman giving me a good rub down. I then helped heave the anchor up and set the sails and they towed my boat back to Gillingham. My home life at this time can be imagined by the fact that after thirty hours absence the only comment from our worthy housekeeper was "Where have you been all day?" No mention of the previous night. "I'm just going out, you had better get yourself some bread and dripping for your tea." She did not reign long — Dad got a weekend leave, discharged her and got another. He was deteriorating rapidly and I believe that these women were just a succession of prostitutes he had picked up in public houses and relied on their good nature to tide things over for a month or two.

In January 1920 we were again without a housekeeper so I was left in charge of my sister and brother to look after the house and fit my schooling in to the best of my ability. I was no more a success than the others and having reached the stage when I spent ten shillings on sweets instead of paying the gas bill and being ashamed to face the old chap, I decided to run away to sea. I was just turned fourteen and still in short trousers. So to begin my campaign I got the next door neighbour to cut down an old pair of my father's trousers to fit me. These were my first long 'uns and I was proud of them.

I had been told that the sea-going barges sometimes loaded cement at Rochester, so one morning towards the end of February 1920, I walked four miles to Rochester, first making enquiries at Ship Pier Chatham, then Blue Boar Pier at

18

Rochester. At the latter pier, somebody told me there were two big barges moored above Cory's coal wharf and just below Rochester Gas Works. I got as near to these two craft as I could from the shore and ascertained that they were the S/B *Lady Rosebery* and the S/B *Eric* both owned by Thomas Watson of Rochester. I hailed these craft and was answered (as I found out later) by Tom Bennett, Mate of the *Lady Rosebery*. I asked if they wanted a cook, and Tom Bennett pointed across the river to the Crown and Quarry Cement Works where a barge was loading and said, "The *Glenmore* over there wants a cook". Although the *Glenmore* was plainly visible, it meant another three mile walk to get to her. I thanked Bennett and plodded on, finally reaching the *Glenmore* at 5 pm.

A tall young fellow of about twenty years of age, was putting hatches on single handed. I asked him civilly if a cook was required, and after eying me doubtfully, no doubt deterred by my youth and smallness, said, "Come on board." I was only four feet nine inches in my boots and stunted through lack of proper food. After scrutinizing me further he said, "Come down the cabin." He preceded me down the companionway and I heard him say "Dad, there's a kid here after a cook's berth." As I entered the cabin I saw my new Skipper for the first time; a huge man over six feet in height, in his fifties and with a greying moustache. This person, Captain George 'Navvy' Brooks promptly said "He's too small." I later found out that they were father and son, and that George, the Mate had been with his dad for five years ever since he left school. George, it transpired later was fed up with keeping two ends — cabin and focsle, clean, cooking, steering and all the innumerable jobs associated with being Mate, and Cook, on a big barge. So he said "Well, we've got to have somebody, if it is only to cook a bit of grub." I was asked if I could cook, and truthfully answered "Yes Sir." I was also asked other questions which I did not answer so truthfully. By the time the interview ended it was agreed that I should join the vessel next morning at nine o'clock and that I would find her at Upnor Buoy. They were left under the impression that I was an orphan, living with an aunt who would only be too pleased to be rid of me. I was to get 12/- per week less breakages and my food. It was weeks later that I learned the meaning of 'less breakages'. In return I was expected to do as I was told. I walked the seven miles back to my home not even having 2d for a tram fare and got indoors about 9 pm. I did not relish the thought of an equally long walk next morning so decided to sail my boat across to Upnor and leave her there. I made a parcel consisting of two blankets, my other shirt and a towel and left a note for my sister telling her to let dad know I had gone, then sneaked out of the house at 6 am on 3 March 1920. When I got to Gillingham Pier I found that there was a strong wind straight down the river and an ebb tide. I could see that I could not fetch Upnor but decided to sail straight across the river, abandon the boat and walk along the foreshore by Cockham Woods to Upnor. I did this and finally got on board at 10 am instead of 9, and was promptly told off for being an hour late. I let the reason for my lateness pass rather than involve myself in further lies. I found out that we were bound to Calais with a 150 tons of cement for cargo, and that as we were not sailing that day the Skipper and Mate were going home and I was to have the boats ashore at 6 am next morning. The Skipper left me out enough food for two meals, locked everything else up and left instructions that I was to scrub the focsle out and pull a riding light up at sunset. I then put them ashore and now had chance to take stock of my new ship.

The *Glenmore* which is still afloat, was one of the crack Channel barges of her day. She was tight and well built, kept spotlessly clean and well found in gear. She was built by Mr J Little a well known character both in his home town and in the City where he was always seen wearing the type of hat known as a 'Mullacutdown'. He built several fine barges at Rochester, including the *Glencoe, Glenhaven, Clenwood, Glendevon, Glenway, Normanhurst, Glenmore* and *Lady Rosebery*. The *Clenwood* was intended to be the *Glenwood* but as the name was already claimed he altered the 'G' to 'C'.

In 1920 the *Glenmore* was owned by Messrs Cunis Limited of Woolwich and Captain Brooks had been her Master since she was built in the year 1903. He had served with Mr Little but had been sold with the ship, I believe in the year 1911. She was 63 tons net register, 78 gross and 86 feet long, 21 wide and a moulded depth of 7 feet 3 inches carrying 150 tons down to her Plimsoll. Incidentally this only left her 9 inches freeboard amidships — not a lot for a craft that was habitually employed in trading to ports in Devon and Cornwall. She had a mule rigged mizen, that is a boom and gaff which instead of being lowered and furled was brailed up to the mast. Her sails when freshly dressed were a deep chocolate colour which, however, soon turned black. With all sails set the white standing jib and jib topsail and sometimes the square sail were in deep contrast to the black foresail, topsail, mainsail and mizen. She had a nice horseshoe-shaped cabin with a companion entrance right aft in the bend of the horseshoe. As one entered the cabin which was built of polished pitch pine, one faced a spring settee athwart the aft bulkhead over which were two long mirrors set in as panels. Just abaft the settee was a door on each side, each of which led to a small stateroom. These staterooms were originally designed for the accommodation of the Master and Mate. But in the *Glenmore,* Captain Brooks reigned aft alone, his berth being on the starboard side and the port side stateroom being used as a larder. In the centre of the cabin was a small drop-leaf table and two chairs, above which was a large skylight which admitted plenty of light and air. Aft again from the stateroom doors on either side were two cupboards flanked at a height of about 20 inches, by two narrow lockers which were used for storing coal. Just clear of the cabin ladder and set against the aft end of the port locker was a small 'Queen' stove. The floor was covered with linoleum with a green and brown motif. This with a green tablecloth set off the deep glow of the pine panelling. The focsle, which was to be my home for the next six and a half years, was not so elaborate, being boarded out with imitation oak grained match boarding. As one came down the focsle ladder and faced forward, one saw the fore peak with two large doors. In this were kept the light headsails, rolling vangs, cement cloths and so on. A small lift-up table was set against these doors and on either side of the focsle was a wide coal locker surmounted by a canvas cot set on a steel frame. The galley stove was set against the fore bulkhead on the starboard side and the Mate used the starboard cot during the winter to be near the stove and would switch over to port side during the hot weather to be away from it. The floor consisted of bare deal boards, with the exception of two sennett mats, and these boards had to be scrubbed white and kept white.

After putting the Skipper and Mate ashore — Brooks being surprised and pleased to find that I could scull a boat with one oar — I prepared myself some dinner and had a good meal. I then scrubbed out the focsle to the best of my ability and generally tidied up. I had been shown where the navigation lights were stowed and how to light the riding light, but not told which halliards to haul it up on. I lit the lamp at sunset and found a rope leading to the topmast head (the flying jib halliards), to which I made fast the lamp and pulled it up clear of the mast head to a height of 60 feet. I was later to learn that in a craft of this size, the rule is not less than 10 feet and not more than 20 feet. I then turned in. About midnight I heard a bumping alongside and went on deck to investigate. I found a small river barge making fast to us and the Skipper on her asked what the riding light was doing up the topmast. "I thought it was a full rigged ship laying on the buoy and was afraid to come alongside in the dark," said he.

I turned in again and was awakened by hearing voices shouting which turned out to be the voices of father and son raised in unison to the cry of "Glenmore Ahoy!" I scrambled into my trousers and sculled ashore to find Brooks Senior in a very bad temper. It was high water and a fair wind and he had been shouting for ten minutes. I was late coming on board yesterday and was late waking up this morning and he was not used to being kept waiting by the boys, and I would have to alter or I would be no good to him etc... With a lump in my throat and tears very near my eyes, I realised that I had not yet created the best of impressions.

As soon as we were back on board the davits were swung out, the boat hoisted, the sails set smart, moorings cast off and my first sea voyage had begun. As soon as we were under way I was ordered below to get breakfast ready while the Mate commenced scrubbing the rails and decks. I was to find unexpected and rigid discipline on board the *Glenmore*. In harbour there were fixed times for meals — breakfast at 8, dinner at 1, tea at 5 and no supper. The Cook was expected to turn out between 6.30 and 7 am, light the focsle fire and while the water in the kettle was getting hot, proceed aft. After rubbing the cabin stove over, and dusting the panelling, I had to lay the table (we had our meals aft) and cook anything there was to be cooked. The Mate had to turn out at the same time and scrub the decks round before breakfast, then the Skipper was called. During breakfast he invariably found fault with the work that had been done the day before and told us what he

The Author in 1921—a seasoned sailor aged 15

The 'Glenmore', with cider from Totnes to London, 1921

George Brooks at the wheel of the 'Glenmore'

expected to be done today. I wondered how the Mate could wake up regularly every morning, because for the first few months due to the unaccustomed labour, I could have slept to the middle of the day. I found that if we were at anchor in a river or roadstead and the Skipper could not see smoke coming from the galley chimney by 7 in the morning, he came stamping for'ard threw about fifteen fathoms of cable over the windlass and then shouted down the focsle hatch "On deck and heave this cable in." If we were moored he would drip a full dip bucket of overboard water down the focsle with a clatter and say, "Turn out, and clean that damned mess up." I learnt to turn out smartly alright.

The wind was West by South, moderate to fresh, and we made a remarkably good passage to Calais. In my innocence, I had not realised that one could be in a foreign country in thirteen hours by sailing barge. We carried our ebb right round the North Foreland and down to the South Goodwin Lightship. The ebb running for three hours longer through the downs than the Thames side of the Foreland, I was kept busy and was too excited to think about sea-sickness, but at 3 pm by the time we were clear of the Goodwins the wind had backed to SW and there was a nasty short jump in the Channel. At 5 pm half channel over, I attempted to walk aft with a full teapot and with the unaccustomed pitch and feeling decidedly groggy, I fell on the deck, teapot as well. If I expected sympathy I soon learned different. I lay on the weather side by the forehorse and to quicken me in picking myself up the Skipper luffed her up a couple of points so that she put some water over her weather bow. He then said in what I thought was a frightening voice, "Pick the teapot up Sonny, and make some more."

We were moored in the West dock at Calais by 7 pm and discharged our cargo of cement the next day. After we were unloaded the weather being dry, the Skipper allowed the Mate to sweep the cement off the decks with a hair broom for the evening on the understanding that there would be a scrub down next morning. After I washed the tea things up, swept the cabin and focsle, I was given permission to go ashore and was advanced five Francs to go with. I did not know at the time that Francs were a hundred to the Pound. I wandered round old Calais, drinking in the foreign smells and talk and the sight of one small tramcar towing two others. I bought some fruit with my five Francs and had a most enjoyable evening.

The voyage back to Rochester was uneventful and we moored on a buoy just below the Crown and Quarry mill about 11 in the morning. The Skipper went ashore to ring up the agents to enquire about the next cargo and was met by a Police Inspector who explained that I had run away from home and school, that they had sent for my father and he would be there very shortly. He was advised to say nothing to me but just see that I did not try to bolt. I was unaware of all this and had not given my past actions a thought. We had just sat down to dinner in the cabin when a voice called down "Alfred." I jumped to my feet and automatically replied "Yes Dad." I must have been a convincing little liar because the Mate turned to the Skipper and said, "Why, his dad is dead." I went on the deck followed by the Skipper. Dad turned to the Police Inspector and said "Well Officer, here's the scallywag; we had better see about getting him ashore." He then proceeded to lecture old Brooks on taking schoolboys away without enquiries and there was a spirited argument. I was a miserable onlooker when the Skipper said, "Well the boy has got £1 due to him, he had better have it." Father said nothing so I took the money and we went ashore. The Policeman shook hands with my father and left us and I had to face up to my father. He said, "What made you do it?" I forget what lamentable reason I gave, but I had a good father for he then said, "We will shake hands; you try and be a better son and I will try and be a better father. Now let us buy some shoes and stockings with that money."

The Spring Term had finished the day previously and there was a fortnight's holiday for Easter. I was still thrilled by my first voyage and persuaded my father to let me go and see Captain Brooks at his home with the view of doing another trip. I found he was a different man ashore, devoted to his family and with a nice house and home. There was a short slack period between cargoes and the *Glenmore* still swung on the buoy off Chatham. They had not shipped a new lad and as Captain Brooks would never leave the vessel without somebody on board, his son, the Mate, had been marooned for two days. He had been allowed to come home for his dinner and fortunately was there when I called. No doubt in his own interest he sided with me, and Captain Brooks reluctantly agreed to my going on board if I would bring my father's written permission. This I obtained and went aboard with George the next day. I was given a list of jobs to do and left to my own devices for four days.

During this period the barge *Thyra* skippered by Captain F Gurr moored alongside and it so happened that I had sawn and chopped a large sack of firewood for use on board. Next day Master and Mate returned with the information that we were loading that day for Lowestoft. I received my first praise that day, Captain Gurr saying, within my hearing, "He is a good boy George, been busy ever since I have been alongside." They never knew that two days previously I had rowed down to Upnor, made the boat fast and had a wonderful day birdsnesting.

CHAPTER 2

Glenmore
and Navvy Brooks

We made an uneventful passage to Lowestoft until we sailed into the harbour. We rounded alongside a large steam trawler moored to the quay; the *Glenmore* still carried a little way and the Captain said, "Jump up and catch a turn Sonny." At this point the trawler's rail was about three feet above my head. I jumped expecting to grip the top of the rail with my fingers but unexpectedly found that the capping surmounting the rail was six inches wide. My fingers slipped and I flopped into the water. As I came to the surface the Skipper's strong right hand reached over and hauled me on board by the scruff of the neck. I had not laced my boots up and one of them had come off and sunk. So that the reward for my first ten days labour was nil.

I had 2/6d in my pocket so next morning thinking I would create a good impression, I slipped out of my cot at 5 am without awakening the Mate and went to the fish market with the intention of buying some fish for breakfast. I had three nice plaice given to me but was so interested in the bustle and excitement of watching the various catches being unloaded that I lost all sense of time. I arrived back on board at 9 am to find the barge alongside the quay discharging. They thought I had run away and instead of praise I had been seeking, I got a devil of a lecture. We discharged and sailed for Rochester.

In the meantime my father had received my school report (a bad one) and had written to the Headmaster explaining my absence. In reply he had been informed that I was not a suitable pupil and that if I failed to return at the end of the Easter vacation it would save the Headmaster the trouble of expelling me. My father told me that I had ruined his pros-

pects and hopes for me and that I could continue along the
road I had started. I was then officially installed 'Cook-
Deckhand' of the good ship *Glenmore*. I had put my age on a
year and was supposed to be fifteen years four months.

The Skipper by then had secured a lucrative contract to last
for three months to carry cement from Rochester to Calais at
one Guinea per ton. There were three other barges with a
similar contract: the *Lady Rosebery*, Captain G Barker; the
Eric, skippered by an old man called Vant; and the *Glenway*,
Captain Dave Brooks, younger brother of my Skipper. The
first two craft at the time were owned by Thomas Watson of
Rochester, and the *Glenway* by a Mr Wilkes of Deal, who also
owned a barge called *Iverna*.

The Mate pinned a written list up in the focsle of my various
duties. It read as follows: "Everyday prepare breakfast. While
waiting for kettle to boil, lay table, rub cabin stove over with
polish, brush and dust cabin panel work, table cloth to be
shaken after each meal and cabin swept after each meal. All
washing up to be done on fore hatches, no dirty pots to be left.
Lamps to be trimmed first thing after breakfast. Tuesdays
and Fridays focsle to be scrubbed out. Cabin to be scrubbed
out on Wednesdays and Saturdays. Cabin and deck brass to
be cleaned on Saturdays. On Thursdays sufficient wood to be
chopped to keep cabin and focsle wood locker full. Wood to
be chopped on a chopping block, and axe to be stowed in
locker. Prepare vegetables and have cooking pot on as soon as
lamps are trimmed. Assist on deck as required. When called
on deck, leave everything and come immediately."

The *Glenmore* was the only barge I knew to set a white linen
tablecloth for meals, and woebetide the unfortunate crew if
they upset a cup of tea. Although I did not realise it at the
time, and for several years for that matter, my choice of the
Glenmore as my first ship, was very lucky. Her Master, one of
the old school of bargemen, was a born seaman, strictly moral
in his habits, abstemious and scrupulously clean. He gave me
the discipline I needed and in his own bullying manner,
taught me my job. He had had very little education and had
difficulty in reading or writing a letter. His son, and in time I
myself, wrote all his business letters; but he knew every inch of
the bottom of the English Channel as well as he knew the surface. His knowledge of forthcoming weather was uncanny. He
would come on deck first thing in the morning, practically

close his left eye, and gaze first aloft and then all round, snuffle at the air like a dog and then give his opinion of the forthcoming day. I seldom knew him to be wrong, and he was certainly more accurate in his own area than the present forecasts from the Meterological Department. He had some quaint sayings. One was "Cleanliness is next to Godliness. I ain't religious," and then paradoxically, "but, by God, I will have things clean." He carried this cleanliness to excess and later in my service under him, I once had to bag the coal up in the coal lockers, take it on deck, scrub the lockers out with hot soda water and when dry paint the interior. After this operation was completed the lockers were refilled with coal.

He used to coin words of his own invention, one of which deserves a place in the King's English. In his pleasanter moments he called me "Jimmy Pippin", but more often than not I was an "obstreperous aggranoying boy". In moments of temper he often hit me but claimed that he treated me like his son. This was true as even his son George in his weaker moments said we were treated like trained dogs. He was very particular about the appearance of his ship and before loading cement each shroud was protected with a canvas cloth six feet long to keep the cement out of the running ropes. All spare mooring ropes were coiled at the back of the mast, the tow rope hoisted on the main sheet block and the whole lot protected by a canvas cover. After a cargo had been loaded these covers had to be taken ashore and thoroughly shaken if the weather had remained dry before being stowed away. If there had been rain they were scrubbed and dried before going below. The decks and rails were then swept with a hair broom. As Third Hand one of my jobs was to follow the Mate around dusting the rails with a small hand brush. Then the real scrub down commenced with the decks being scrubbed thoroughly; he would only allow the rails to be mopped unless the cement was stubborn, then they had to be done with a hand scrubber and swab. A long-handled bass mop consisting of two feet long unlaid strands of coir rope was kept for washing the anchor cable as it was hove on board. If we anchored in blue clay, after the thickest of it had been mopped off, the cable had to be flaked along the foredeck and scrubbed before being stowed.

Later when I was Mate he had a habit which used to drive me nearly frantic. I would religiously scrub and mop from for'ard to aft for anything from four to six hours and just as I was about to draw the last pail of water he would say, "That will do for today, you can finish it in the morning." Failing this, he would let me finish and then get a pail of water, stalk round with a critical eye and give a little scrub here and there with a scrubber. As Cook I was allowed ashore after obtaining permission every other evening whilst in port. He had to be in a good humour to allow both the Mate and myself ashore together.

We finally loaded our cargo and sailed in the company of the *Lady Rosebery* and *Glenway*. I found I had to ask his permission to go on board another barge for a yarn, certain craft being taboo for fear of bringing bugs back on board. For the same reason I was not allowed to exchange books with other ships. After our arrival at Calais I was allowed ashore in the evening, being advanced a whole ten Francs. There were still British troops in Calais and seeing a queue of Tommies outside a large building I joined them thinking it was a picture house. One of the Tommies said to another "What does this little French tyke want?" I then said "I am English, mister, and I'm going to the pictures." He had the the grace to look shamed when he said "This isn't a picture house, sonny, you get up to the other part of town." I afterwards found I had queued up outside a Government brothel.

At that time there were a number of thugs round the docks of the northern ports of France, and the Masters and Mates always used to go ashore in pairs or larger numbers because two bargemen and other seamen had been fished out of the dock after being stunned and robbed. My Skipper evidently considered I was too small to run any risk for he never stopped me from going ashore for this particular reason. At the time I was a polite and well-spoken lad and I assume this was rather a novelty in the barges because other Skippers began to take an interest in me and would talk to me when they would not think of lowering their dignity by mixing with their own crews. Toward the end of this contract I had a narrow escape from death. We were moored empty alongside the Southern Quay in the West dock of Calais at the time. A large three masted auxiliary schooner, the *Kobenhaven* of Copenhagen, attempted to turn round and get out of the dock on the high tide. Whether the Master had imbibed too freely I do not know, but he was late and the dockmen were closing the lock gates. There was a lot of shouting which caused me to look up and see the schooner coming head first for us amidship at a good speed. Our Skipper was in the town somewhere and George the Mate was talking to the Master of another barge about three lengths away. He came running along the quay shouting "Put a fender in." By now the other ship's jibboom was right across us. I grabbed a fender and stood by for the blow. At the last moment my heart failed me and I stepped on one side. She had clipper bows and just as I dodged aside they let go an eight cwt anchor, smack on to our deck which just grazed my right arm. She cut halfway through our port gunwale and covering board and squeezed the old *Glenmore* like a concertina for as she rebounded half our hatches fell down the hold.

Captain Brooks had the other ship detained until he obtained a guarantee of payment for damage received. The next day the Master of the *Kobenhaven* took him ashore, filled him with champagne and offered him a £50 bribe to ignore the damage. In Brooks he tackled the wrong man. He returned on board in the afternoon full of free champagne—one of the few times I was to see him the worse for drink—but as adamant as ever.

He had found fault with most of my work for the two previous days so I indulged in a boyish revenge. As soon as he returned on board he went to sleep on the settee. I crept down the cabin ostensibly to get a pail of water, the water tank being in the spare stateroom. I obtained a feather, hid in the stateroom then put my arm out and proceeded to tickle him under the nose. He grunted and half turned so I got bolder and trailed the feather in his ear and up and down his face. He took several ineffectual slaps at himself without opening his eyes and finally said, "Curse the flies," and staggered on deck without realising I was in the stateroom. Childish, but it gave me great satisfaction. I went on deck and he returned to his interrupted nap. When I called him for tea in a mood of drunken benevolence he said to the Mate, "He's a good little boy George, give him sixpence."

As I have said previously, there were three other barges on this particular contract. Captain George Barker, Master of the *Lady Rosebery* was Bradley's crack Skipper at that time. During the 1914-18 War he had run mostly between Southampton and St Malo in the little boomie *Lord Rosebery*. Most of the Skippers had nicknames by which they were known to each other, and most appropriate most of them were. George Brooks was known as 'Navvy' and his brother Dave, Master of the *Glenway* as 'Weary'. The Master of the *Glencoe* at that time was known as 'Slippery Jim'.

By this time I had made friends with the Cook of the *Glenway*, Bill Pope, now Master of one of John Knight's tugs of Rochester. One evening, us two lads wandered into a cafe frequented by all the skippers and mates, and known as 'Gaby's'. Our two Skippers were seated inside and mine was none too pleased to see me in there. He said "What do you want boy?" When I explained that we had come in for two grenadines, a harmless syrup, he was more friendly. There was a young daughter of the house, aged fifteen. The Skipper jocularly said, "I have brought you a sweatheart from England, Harriet." The pert young miss looked at me and in excellent English said, "What that little boy? He needs to go back to school again." I only had the one grenadine.

Due to the damage caused by the *Kobenhaven*, Captain Brooks decided to return to the firm's headquarters and slipway at Woolwich for repairs and a general overhaul. While on the 'Ways', I discovered that W R Cunis had another 'Jimmy Little' built coaster, the *Normanhurst*, ten tons larger than the *Glenmore*. Captain Brooks always said that the *Glenmore* was built from the odds and ends left over from the *Normanhurst*.

Besides these two craft there was a fleet of river barges consisting of the *Glendevon, Terror, G W Teaser, Torment,* three little ninety tonners, the *Toots, Wumps* and *Doddles,* and an old swim-headed barge, the *Dawcy,* completed the fleet. The *Normanhurst* was skippered by young Alf Lutchford as distinct from his father old Alf, Master at the time of the S/B *Shamrock.* There was also an uncle old Dick Lutchford, also a bargemaster. The master of the *Glendevon* was 'Black' Jack Whiting, who at the beginning of the century had been in command of various sailing colliers running from the North to Whitstable. One of his commands was the old Whitstable-built *Lily.* She was a round stern boomie and was later converted into a 'spreetie' without much success for she was very slow and would more often mis-stay than not.

Like everything else done on board the *Glenmore* our overhaul was thorough. The sails were taken ashore to be repaired and dressed, then the rigging stripped from the spars

SAILORMAN

and all the spars placed on the shore on separate pairs of trestles to be scraped, sandpapered, oiled, sized and varnished. By this method every block and tackle was examined when we rerigged the vessel. Captain Brooks was highly thought of by his employers but was very independent. During this overhaul he was describing slackness in the various bearings on the steering gear to Mr. Ralph Cunis. He said, "There's friction here Governor, and friction here and friction there." Mr Cunis said, "Friction is all balls Brooks, you mean play." Captain Brooks replied, "I don't know about play but it won't b. . . . . . well work and I want it altered."

We looked very smart when we were once more ready for sea and loaded a cargo of cattle cake from London to Poole, Dorset. On the passage to Poole, when below Beachy Head, with a smart breeze from the NNE and smooth water, the Mate was at the wheel while the Skipper was having a watch below. The Mate said to me, "I will give you a half-a-crown if you will go and turn the Bob" (the ship's house flag at the topmast head). I had not yet been higher than the crosstrees but I had climbed many trees when bird-nesting, and it seemed easy money. The *Glenmore* was at a nice steady angle, and I climbed the rigging and then up the topsail hoops with ease. I turned the flag around and then returned to the deck. He then said "If you go up the rigging, climb out along the head rope of the mainsail, and slide down the vang, I will give you another 2/6d." This was more difficult. I lay my belly across the headrope, and hunched myself about a third of the way out, and found I was gazing down at the sea, clear outside the ship's side. I gave in and returned down the rigging to be informed that as I had failed to do my latter task, I would not get the 2/6d. for turning the flag round. It was a dirty trick, but all experience.

While at Poole I saw a full rigged ship flying the Italian flag, loading ball clay from lighters towed down from Wareham, and also first met Captain Frank 'Cully' Teovil, then Master of the S/B *George and Eliza,* and later Master of F T Everard's *Cambria.* From Poole we proceeded to Portland to load stone for London. This cargo consisted of blocks varying from one to ten tons in size and was loaded by men using low geared hand cranes. Loading these huge blocks was an art in itself. To get them under the cupboards and wings they used to land them on wooden rollers and jack them in with hand

32

jacks. While doing this the loaders used to sing a song or dirge to synchronize their movements. To the best of my memory it went something like this: "Jack him up, Get him straight, Round boys Round. Edge him up, In he goes, Round boys Round." The stone would then flop off the rollers in the position required. We carried a bag of wooden scotches to chock up awkwardly shaped stones to stop them rocking at sea. These were also used later for chocking up pipes of Devonshire cider from Totnes.

Stone was not a popular cargo, for you were only paid on the cubic footage that could be obtained when the blocks were cut square and barges used to carry about twenty tons in the hundred for nothing. One of the Mate's duties during the hot summer months was to slosh hundreds of buckets of overboard water on the decks to prevent the seams from opening up. This had to be done after sunset, and if he wanted the evening on shore, it had to be done when he returned on board. Our cargo of stone was for a wharf at Putney in London, which meant that the vessels bowsprit had to be unrigged, and the masts lowered to enable us to pass under the various bridges. We unrigged at Woolwich, and towed to our berth. I was allowed to sub to the extent of 5/- per week, but I never received the balance of my wages until the barge had completed the round trip to London. This sometimes was nearly two months. I had managed to save enough to buy a decent navy blue suit, my first real suit of long 'uns, some underwear and shoes and was at last able to go home looking decent and already two inches taller.

My aunt, Dad's sister, was keeping house and I soon realised that from her point of view I was unwelcome — being the 'bad boy' of the family, although, God knows, none of us had anything to be proud of. My father was still on the HMS *Gibraltar* at Portland, and I did not have the opportunity of displaying my finery to him. I returned on board after my day at home, and we proceeded to Beckton and loaded a cargo of pitch for Dunkirk.

I was still interested in the various cargoes, and although it was a particularly hot day, spent some hours as opportunity served, watching the lumps of pitch slide into the hold. The dockers all wore muslin over their faces. I was to find out why the next day. The fine particles of pitch flying through the air had settled on all the exposed parts of me, and combined with the heat of the sun next day, I literally pealed and was in great pain. When we arrived at Dunkirk we found there was a dock strike, and we lay a fortnight waiting to discharge.

During this period quite a fleet of barges collected: among others the S/B *Major,* Captain Steccles and the S/B *Alaric*, Captain George Wynn. During this period the two captains previously mentioned were involved in a curious incident. They were returning from the Casino at Malo one night, when from a clump of trees on the right, a shot rang out and a man in front of them on the road fell dead. They ran to render first-aid but finding the man dead, they were foolish enough to feel in his pockets to find some means of identifying him. While doing this two gendarmes came along, and they were prompt-ly arrested. They had difficulty in satisfying the authorities of their innocence, and were lucky to escape a charge of murder.

As I lay on board at night, I slept wrapped up in the foresail, it being too hot to sleep below, it was quite common to hear shots and screams or moans. It must have been totally lawless there. During this time I had wandered round the docks and found a huge dump of army lorries and motor cars guarded by four ex-London policemen, who had been discharged in the London Police strike just previously. They were camped in a big hooded army lorry. They were quite friendly and I visited them on several evenings, all carried revolvers slung at their hip. One evening it was getting dark; I wanted to get back on board and one of them volunteered to drive me in a car they were using. We had not proceeded very far when we met six drunken Frenchmen, who joined hands and stood across the width of the road. They were out for trouble and my ex-policeman after sounding his horn in vain, and not wanting to drive over them, pulled up. He got out of the car to reason with them, and they crowded round him. One directly behind him raised a big bottle to hit him over the head. As I had done at the pictures at images, I now yelled "Look behind you!" He turned drawing his revolver, and shot the Frenchman in the leg. He then backed into the car brandishing his revolver and drove through them. For a fourteen year old, I was certainly seeing life. I do not know the results of this incident, because I was not allowed ashore any more at Dunkirk, after telling my story.

The pitch finally had to be unloaded at night with hose pipes running on it as it had congealed into one solid mass. We

34

Glenmore and Navvy Brooks

sailed for England, this time passing outside the East Goodwin, and straight for the North Goodwin lightship. While passing the Goodwins, Captain Brooks told me that his cousin had commanded the *Glenavon*, and had followed the boomie *Corinthian* across from Antwerp when they both went ashore on the East Goodwin in an Easterly gale. They grounded within a hundred yards of each other and all the crew of the *Corinthian* were saved by the Deal lifeboat, and the crew of the *Glenavon* were drowned. I remember Brooks saying, "Snuffy ought to have known better than to follow another man."

Food on board the *Glenmore* was good and plentiful: while in harbour we would have a big piece of rib of beef or a leg of mutton roast with vegetables one day and cold with the fried-up remains of the vegetables the following day; also a big currant pudding, the remains of this also being sliced and eaten next day; there was also a fore-end of bacon in the spare stateroom and if we did not have cold meat for breakfast the Skipper used to cut rashers of bacon off a quarter of an inch thick. We used to carry a salt meat crock and before proceeding to sea the Skipper would buy about twenty pounds of flank of beef. This used to be in four joints. The first was roasted fresh, and the others put in brine in the crock. He had one foible, when ordering stores: he never included bottles of sauce, saying "Good grub doesn't need any pilots."

At sea, the routine was the same: cook one day and fry up the next. Sometimes we had a huge meat pudding. On these days the cooking pot had to be boiling at 8 am and the meat duff had to have at least four hours boiling. Most of the cooking was done in a two gallon cast iron pot, vegetables as well and they were all the tastier for it. The only thing Captain Brooks was mean with was bread. Consequently our bread was always a day old, and sometimes a week. If we had no stale bread when buying any I had to ask for the previous day's baking. For breakfast or tea, he would cut two thick slices off and put them on my plate. If I was hungry and ate them quickly, he would look at me and in a ferocious voice say, "You don't want any more bread, do you Boy?" I used to swallow and invariably say, "No thank you Sir!"

We next loaded a cargo of cement from Rochester to Totnes, Devon, and from there loaded cider for Free Trade Wharf, London. While on passage to Totnes, we anchored in the

SAILORMAN

'Gore above Margate', with strong SW winds for three days. While at anchor we caught two large bowls full of Whiting and Whiting Pout. The first evening I cooked some for tea. During the meal Brooks looked up and said, "There is no need to be greedy, Boy! There is plenty of time." I promptly pushed my plate away, and refused to eat my tea. When the meal was finished, I commenced to clear the table, when he said, "Put that plate of fish in the stateroom, you can have it for breakfast." I refused to eat it at breakfast time and went without food for two days. I finally gave in and started eating the fish, although it stank. As soon as he saw he had broken my will, he said, "Alright, put it on one side, and get something else to eat." My God, I was trained alright.

I had my revenge a little later. We had a leg of salt pork in the meat crock and when I was told to cook it, I put it straight into a pot of boiling water without washing it. Immediately hundreds of huge maggots came to the surface. I skimmed them off, and said nothing. At dinner I said I did not like pork, and gloated while he ate his.

The cabin table contained a locker which was filled with big ships' biscuits. We occasionally ran out of bread while on passage, and had recourse to these biscuits. They must have been there for years, because if you knocked them on the table, big black weevils fell out of them, but we used to eat them. We were not allowed supper in harbour, but at sea we had it at 10 pm. After clearing away, and washing and sweeping up, I was allowed to have my pillow on the locker and lay down. We were not allowed to undress and sleep while under way.

When I first started going down channel, the wreck of the full rigged ship *Preussen*, still had four masts standing. She went ashore under the South Foreland after breaking adrift from tugs. Previous to this, she had been in collision with the Newhaven-Dieppe mail boat. After the collision tugs attempted to tow her to London which ended her career. She was reported to have had a cargo of pianos, unless my leg was being pulled at this time.

The next voyage I experienced the terrors of Portland Race in a breeze. We had discharged a cargo of cement in Exmouth Dock and as there was very little wind, the Mate had persuaded his father to stop until the morning tide, to enable him to have an evening ashore. We sailed the following morning empty, bound to Portland to load another cargo of stone. During the day the wind freshened from the East. It was dark by the time we approached the Bill and there being a strong head wind the Skipper would not attempt to tack up in the narrow smooth water strip close under the Bill. It was pitch dark, we had the mizen stowed and the head of the topsail down, and broken water came on board from all directions. The Skipper stood one side of the wheel, and the Mate on the other. I cowered back on the starboard quarter hanging on to the aft davit as tightly as I could. I was so frightened that I tried to say the Lord's Prayer, and could not remember it. This upset me more because I thought I was going to drown without saying my prayers. The Skipper was nagging at the Mate, and blaming him for the fact that we had not sailed the previous evening. He was a determined man and would not turn back. We eventually got far enough to the East to be out of the broken water and sailed by the Shambles light and into harbour.

By now I was well acquainted with the meaning of 'less breakages'. It meant that every time I was unlucky enough or careless enough to break a lamp glass while cleaning it, or lose a bucket over the side, I had to pay for two. Incidently I also had to supply a bill when I made these purchases, which was no doubt later presented to the owner for repayment. Sometimes my 12/- weekly wage was sadly depleted.

The owner never queried the cargoes that the Captain fixed or his movements. When we arrived in harbour he would send them a postcard informing them of the fact. When bound down Channel from London with strong South to West winds, he would often sail up the River Medway, and anchor on Hoo Flats within a quarter of a mile of his home. Sometimes we would lay there for a week with loaded ship.

We carried a sharp, light twelve foot boathook in the mizen rigging. With this I was expected to stab and pick up any drifting wood or boxes. Sometimes we picked up quite large planks. These were stowed down the hold and I had to saw these and other pieces into eight inch lengths in my spare time, and bag them up. When we sailed round to Hoo Flats, a horse and cart would come to the quayside—there was an old brick-making wharf there— and ashore would go my planks and bags of chocks destined for 'Glen Cottage', the residence of my respected Captain. The vessel was only afloat for about an hour each tide on the Flats and would ride out any breeze in safety. After the cabin and focsle had been scrubbed out, rather than leave me to my own devices, he used to take me home. I found out that on these excursions, I was expected to help clean out chicken houses and whitewash them, scrub old cement sacks and whitewash fruit trees in season.

During my first winter at sea, on one occasion, we sheltered in the outer harbour at Dover with numerous other barges and various ketches and schooners, for three weeks. There was a succession of S and SW, gales and one day with a severe southerly gale and seas coming right over the breakwater, a German three-masted schooner tried to enter the western entrance of the harbour. Her name was the *Wesser* and she hit the eastern arm of the entrance, knocked her jibboom out and missed the harbour. Her crew could be seen aloft clinging to the rigging. By some miracle the backwash or rebound kept her off the breakwater and she went right round to the eastern entrance without touching. There the tug *Lady Duncannon* took her in tow. As the tug pulled her head to wind, her foremast and fore topmast crashed to the deck. The only casualty was one man with a broken arm.

We finally mustered fifteen spreeties, two boomies, three ketches, two topsail schooners and a barquentine all bound to various Channel ports. The wind was NE, light. By the time we were in the vicinity of the Royal Sovereign lightship, the wind had veered to SSE and it was thick with snow. The barquentine, schooners and ketches held their luff and continued down Channel, but playing follow the leader, all the barges ran for Newhaven. We were the first in, and moored without trouble. The S/B *Scot* rolled his spreet out but entered safely; the *Gravelines* ran on a gridiron and sank with her cargo of barley; Everard's *Cambria*, Captain Milton, stuck his bowsprit through the wheelhouse of the *Leonard Piper*, then skippered by Captain Frank Day, Senior; in turn, this pulled the *Cambria's* topmast out (but he was only bound to Shoreham); finally, the *Portland May* skippered by 'Dosher' fell athwart the *Glenmore's* head and her bowsprit jammed between two open piles in the quay.

'Dosher' was a remarkable little man, as agile as a cat and proud of it. On this particular occasion the crew of the *May* led a stern line on to the *Glenmore*, took the weight on it and 'Dosher' went out onto the bowsprit end in an attempt to push

'Gravelines I' sunk at Newhaven, winter 1920-21

A rare photograph of 'Hibernia'—at Bridport in 1930

'Royalty' and 'Cambria' towing into Great Yarmouth

it clear. He was standing on the end of the bowsprit, a nine inch spar about twenty eight foot long when the line broke. Our Skipper shouted out, "You're adrift Dosh," and without hesitation 'Dosher' turned, spread his arms wide and ran inboard along the full length of the bowsprit.

Our Skipper ordered me aloft to stow the topsail. I endeavoured to do so but it was billowing out so much and my hands were so cold and lifeless, that when I did succeed in passing the furling line round it I could not tell the feel of my fingers from the rope. I was aloft for ten minutes and then came down and said, "I can't do it, Sir!" He came storming along the deck saying, "There is no such word in the dictionary as 'can't'. Get aloft." He followed me up the rigging, showed me how to get above the topsail and ride it down with him on top of me, and then he made me hold the furling line while his hands guided mine round the sail. It was only his weight and experience that stowed the sail, but he said, "Don't let me hear you use the word 'can't' again. It isn't allowed on this ship."

After several days the fleet set sail once more and ran into more trouble. We were bound to Frater, Portsmouth. The wind was strong easterly, and it was dirty with visibility down to a quarter of a mile. The *Glenmore* and *Normanhurst* ran abreast, one on the port gybe and one on the starboard. We both passed over the top of the Owers shoal, fortunately missing the most shallow water and succeeded in getting inside the Isle of Wight. Some of the barges missed the Island altogether. 'Dosher' lost his mizen mast. Captain Phil French of the S/B *Cetus* found himself abreast of St Catherines Point and attempted to tack into the western end of the Solent. His Mate and Cook-Steward were washed over the side and drowned; thereupon he bore away and anchored just below Christchurch Ledge and was later assisted into Poole.

While at anchor in Dover Bay, the only time we were allowed ashore was to get food and water. The boat was lowered from the davits at some quiet period when there was not too much sea on the beach. The Mate would land on the beach and chase up to the town after stores, while the Third Hand kept the boat afloat and waited for him. This taught us the art of beaching a boat, the main thing being to keep either head or stern to sea and then go in on a roller. As soon as we returned on board it was "up boat and gripe her in". I have swung

SAILORMAN

within three cables of the shore and not been allowed to land for a month.

The average barge only carried about 100 to 150 gallons of fresh water and this was carefully conserved. All vegetables were cleaned in overboard water, and if there were no greasy dishes, the crockery was washed up in overboard water. During rain storms, buckets and breakers were placed at various strategic points to catch the water running off the spars. If really short of water, we had to row to various barges borrowing breakers until we had amassed as many as we could then row inside the Prince of Wales Pier, fill them up, return, empty them in the tank, and then take back the borrowed breakers. Before letting us use the breakers of other barges, Brooks made us chain and rinse them out. This meant inserting about a fathom of small chain in the bung hole, allow a gallon of water to enter, and then shake the breaker vigourously and rinse out.

I first became acquainted with 'Dosher' when borrowing breakers in Dover Bay. George, our Mate had shown me how to make a rather elaborate bow fender for the ship's boat. I first spliced a small thimble neatly in each end of a piece of tarred 1½ inch rope about fifteen inches long. Then built a core of bass yarns round it, so that it was about three inches in diameter at the middle, and tapered off to nothing at the ends. Then I cut about forty pieces of spun yarn to the length of the fender and bound them on, over and under, with another piece of spunyarn. As the fender tapered, various strands of spunyarn were discarded and a neat finish made with whipping twine. 'Dosher' was one of the old school of bargemen also, equally as clean as my Captain. Where he differed was in physique—and the fact that he was excitable and given to the use of foul language. He was a typical Cockney, and boasted to me, "Four feet one and a half inches I was when I went to sea, and had to stand on a soap box to steer." His Mate had been with him for eight years, and the work on board was done in a continuous round of abuse from one to the other. I sculled alongside the *May* one morning to borrow breakers, and 'Dosher' immediately saw the new fender on our boat. He said to his Mate, Jerry, "There's seamanship for you, you blankety blank. A fifteen year old boy can show you up." This was a libel, for Jerry could make any known knot or splice and used to splice all the new wire work in on the *May*.

One morning, when I was emptying ashes over the side before breakfast, I saw 'Dosher' climb the rigging, walk up the topmast with his hands on the halliards and feet on the spar. He then climbed on to the topmast truck, stood up, and balanced without any support on the six inch disc of the truck eighty-five feet above the deck. He them clambered down from the topmast head and slid down the backstay to the deck. When later I had chance to ask for the reason of this display, he merely said, "To show those other blankety blanks that it can be done." There was a large fleet in the harbour at the time and I assume I was not the only spectator.

When the topmast on the *May* was scraped or oiled, the method for going aloft was for Jerry to be seated in a bosun's chair, made fast to the flying jib halliards with his feet on one crosstree while 'Dosher' stood on the other crosstree grasping the other part of the halliards. The Third Hand stood on the deck holding onto the same part. 'Dosher' would jump off the crosstree, and the Third Hand pulled him easily to the deck while Jerry went up. The Third Hand was the nephew of 'Dosher' and we became good friends. He also was a Cockney, and used to pronounce 'th' as 'v'. He once said to me, "Don't you talk nice. I wish I could say Muvver and Favver like you do." Jerry taught me how to wash my shirts properly. He would recite a little rhyme: "First the cuffs and then the breast, and it doesn't matter a damn about the rest." My last sight of these two stalwarts together was one at each end of a cross-cut saw, sawing a log of wood on a trestle placed on the deck of the *May*. They as usual were hurling abuse at each other, but the rhythm of the saw never faltered.

Dosher's eyesight began to fail shortly after and although he had remained a batchelor into his fifties he very wisely married and retired. Jerry remained and after taking charge of the *May* and drinking himself out of her, became Mate under me eight years later. He was a good seaman, but absolutely unreliable when in harbour. I found it a good plan when he was Mate with me to hold his money for several weeks and then let him have it all at once. He would go on the spree and report back when he was spent out.

Until now I had only come into contact with the Channel barges, but the following summer I found there was another race of bargemen known as 'Essexmen'. These mostly worked on the East Coast. When freights slacked off in the summer, a few of them would come seeking down Channel. There were good men but 'Navvy' referred to them comtemptuously as 'Reed Sparrows' or 'Butterflies'. One summer afternoon as we sailed from Dover bound west, he observed the *Glenrosa*, Captain Cullum and *Major* Captain Steccles, rounding the South Foreland and remarked, "The sun is out, here come the butterflies."

That summer I saw the unusual spectacle of three barges passing Portland Bill, commanded by the three Brooks brothers. *Glenmore* bound to Totnes, *Glenway* bound to Plymouth, and the *Venta* formerly *Jachin* bound to Torquay. At Dartmouth I saw the boomie *Lord Hamilton* with a cargo from Liverpool. She was then skippered by Jack Josh, but was later lost on the North Goodwin with the loss of her Skipper, Captain Farnes and crew. Josh is still going strong to this day, a big experienced man who has had good ships, but never remained many years with one firm. While running up Channel with a cargo of cider on this trip, we passed Tommy Harker in the *Challenge* banging to windward across the West Bay against a strong westerly wind. He was a big jolly man with a heart like a lion and the reputation for going to sea in any weather. 'Navvy' always said Tommy would drown himself. This unfortunately happened two years later, through no fault of Tommy's. He was cut down off Jersey in dense fog by a steamship and he and his wife were drowned, but the Mate was saved.

Freights were scarce in the summer of 1922 and the rates were falling sharply. I remember 'Navvy's' indignation when we loaded a cargo of Portland stone, on finding that Tommy Cullum in *Glenrosa* and Freddie Gurr then in charge of the new *Marie May* had fixed the same day as himself and cut the rate by 4/- per ton. That year several of us were caught in a westerly breeze. Teddy Prior's *Lady Helen*, went ashore at Dungerness; the *Convoy* and others anchored in Eastbourne Roads and the *Convoy* pounded so heavily on the seas, that she had to be refastened; but the *Glenmore, Glenway* and *Major* succeeded in getting as far as the 'Park' off Selsea Bill and rode out the gale for twenty-eight hours. The *Major* attempted to get under way a day later, but he was evidently sheeting his mainsail home without a mousing on the mainsheet block. They had got the mainsail practically set when the block unhooked. The huge block and sail were snaking through the air rendering it impossible for the crew to get foreward without risk of having their heads knocked off. The mainsail just blew to pieces and they did not get under way.

In 1923 my father left the land of the living and my aunt sold the house and home up, took my sister and brother to bring them up with her at Plymouth and left me flat. I was now really on my own.

I had discovered another unpleasant fact previous to this. At all ports west of Portland Bill crews were expected to work cargo when loaded with cement. This meant rigging a gin block aloft on the topsail halliard and sheet and erecting a hand dolly winch on the quay. On board the *Glenmore* Captain Brooks paid a man at the rate of 4d per ton to sling the 2 cwt jute bags in the hold, and the Mate and I hove them up on to carts or lorries. I had to prepare my vegetables overnight, get an early breakfast and put the pot on, and then proceed to heave on the winch all day. When the others knocked off for 'elevenses', or morning break, I had to nip below and put my dinner on. After being on the winch all the afternoon I had to prepare tea, sweep the ends up and wash all the crocks ready for a clear start next morning—and I was still only getting 12/- per week. I had asked for a rise but the Skipper had given me a lecture on all my faults without mentioning any good points that I possessed. I was still friends with Bill Pope and he was still in the *Glenway*. In June 1923, George was promoted to Skipper of the *Normanhurst*. Captain Brooks doubtfully agreed to give me a trial as Mate, on condition that I got Bill Pope to come with me and shared the wages. This we did and I became Mate of the *Glenmore* at the age of seventeen.

CHAPTER 3

Mate
of the Glenmore

I was proud of my promotion, and did my best to satisfy Captain Brooks. But there was no satisfying him. If a job was done well there was no comment, but if anything was left undone, he would nag for hours. All the years I was with him I never received one word of praise.

That year I was to observe several examples of his unerring weather lore. We sailed from the Thames bound to Poole and just before dark anchored in the 'Gore'. There was a fresh SW wind and rain squalls. He said "Don't give her too much cable, and sleep lightly, this wind will be NE by morning." I watched Margate lights for a while and remarked to Bill Pope "Our clever Captain will come unstuck this time." At 4 am he came dashing forward with the order "Heave up." There was a smart breeze from the NE. I have known him after being under way for several hours with a nice breeze and thick fog to say, "Have a cast with the lead boy, you have got seven fathoms." He was always right: it was not a query, but a statement of fact.

One night, with a strong southerly wind and thick with rain coming up channel, he had me standing by the lee quarter board just abaft the leeboard winch, sounding the lead and up to my knees in swirling water. The lead line consisted of a 7 lb conical shaped piece of lead with a cavity in the bottom, which one could fill with grease and when hauled up and examined one could judge the type of bottom. The method of use was to hold about two fathoms of slack line in one hand and swing the lead with the other hand as far forward as possible. Then let the line slide through the fingers until it touched bottom. After about an hour of being told "Have a cast boy, you've got eight fathoms or six fathoms or five," I said "If you know what water there is, what am I wasting my time for?" He replied "There are as many hills under there as there are on the land. When you learn where they are, you will know where you are." This was a lesson I learned well, and later as Master in fine weather and on a rising tide, I would sound across shoals, out of the fairway, to find future short cuts.

Shortly after being made Mate, we passed through St Albans Race, with a west going tide and a fresh SW wind. We were loaded with Portland stone and found that we had got a 'Rocker'. A ten ton block was not evenly stowed and with every roll of the vessel it thumped heavily on the ceiling. Brooks was worried about it going through her bottom. We proceeded as far as Ryde, IOW and there anchored and crawled about among the cargo looking for the culprit. Brooks forced one corner up slightly with a heavy oak mast prop, which enabled me to get a chock under it. After the operation was completed he vented his temper by throwing the mast prop onto another stone, it ricochetted and broke two of his toes. Much to my satisfaction he could not walk for four days. Previous to this we had been in the company of the S/B *Opal* when she foundered in Margate Roads loaded with Portland stone. It wanted a good barge to carry it. The boomie *Justice* also sank off Deal loaded with grain. The crew had gone ashore and a strong wind came on the land so that they could not get off and she just foundered for want of pumping. About this time the *Tintarra* had her topmast rent in two by lightning when loaded with a cargo of barrelled sprats from Brightlingsea to Poole.

That autumn was a stickler for SW and W winds. We loaded a cargo of cement from Rochester to Exeter and were ten weeks getting down channel. We had a fortnight in the Downs and then got as far as Beachy Head when the wind again came strong from the WSW. We ran back and anchored in the East Bay at Dungeness and had the company of five other barges. Captain Brooks always made us keep anchor watch in an open roadstead, having once been cut down by a full rigged ship while at anchor under Dungeness. While sheltering behind the Ness we had two anchors down with 60 fathoms of cable on each. It fined away on a Saturday and we hove the second anchor on board. At 4 am Sunday morning he came forward and said, "Your watch. When it gets daylight, lead that cable aft, take the turns out of it and chip some of the rust off." It was the old hell ship motto all over again: "For Six Days Thou Shalt Labour All That Thou Are Able, And On The Seventh Holystone The Decks And Scrape The Cable." Next morning there was a light wind from the east and a soft rain. He gave the order "Under way." While we were heaving the anchor up a full rigged ship under full canvas glided by to the west. Much to my surprise and disgust the next order was "Pull your sheets in tight and get that boat as high as she will come and lash her inboard." We then started tacking back towards Dover. He shouted until he had roused somebody on the next barge at anchor, and then proceeded. I muttered various remarks to Bill about the Skipper having lost his nerve, and that he did not want us to earn any money. I had yet to learn. We had only progressed about four miles when looking astern I said, "The other barges have got the heads of their topsails down and are coming up fast." The Skipper gave the order to down topsail and stow the mainsail. This was done smartly, and within ten minutes we were running before a 100 mile an hour gale. By the time we were abreast of Dover there was too much sea to take the harbour and I saw a big old comber racing along about a quarter of a mile inside of us, which seemed to be twenty feet above the other waves. I found out after that this particular wave had washed four railway carriages off the Prince of Wales Pier at Dover. We managed to anchor in the Downs where we pulled a taut one on two anchors. We had not been anchored many hours when my full rigged ship was towed past us dismasted.

After a lapse of a week we once more got as far as Dover. There we had another three weeks in company with numerous other barges. One day the wind came from the north and four barges mustered and proceeded west. Brooks said, "Let them go; there will be more than they want before the day is out." The wind backed to the NNW and blew a hurricane. One of the barges the *Venta* (Phil Brooks now had the *Velonia*) was dismasted off Beachy Head. Her crew were taken off by a passing steamer. The *Ardwina* was abandoned in mid-channel, and Everard's boomie *Evelyn*, last seen passing through the Downs, disappeared without trace. The little boomie *Garson* managed to get to Newhaven, but so great had been the strain on the rigging, that the wire shroud lanyards had crushed right through the deadeyes on the shrouds. We finally arrived at Exeter on Armistice Day, 11 November. We loaded barytes from Exeter for London, and finished discharging this cargo ten days before Christmas. The Skipper came back from the 'City' to say we were fixed to load wheat from the Surrey Dock to Southampton. I had visions of Christmas rolling about off Dover, but we went down channel, discharged our wheat, on to Portland, loaded stone and were tied up at Putney by Christmas Eve.

I was now well developed physically, and doing a man's work. If Brooks had been more humane I would have been happy. He suffered from stomach trouble, which I believe made him so irascible. At home he was a different man, with a devoted wife. But even then, he would be like a lamb for a week and then start kicking mats out of the way, saying "Pack my bag, I'm off." At one period, he drove me so frantic with his nagging, that I seriously thought of committing suicide, by jumping off the cross trees with the flying jib halliards round my neck. During 1924 we loaded our usual cement for Totnes, inside of Dartmouth, and cider back. Upon arrival at Totnes, the Skipper went home. Bill and I hove the cargo of cement out. Three days at fifty tons a day. The weekend intervened and we then took three days loading the cider. During this time we managed to scrape and oil the topmast and mizen boom, paint both the staterooms out and tar round the ship's sides. The Skipper returned and without any comment on his part, we towed down to Dartmouth. The wind was NE so we sheltered in Dartmouth next day. As it was a bright day without being told, we removed the spare pump handles and lumber irons from where they were stowed in the wheelbox and chipped and painted them. Then I painted the interior of the wheelbox. We carried two kicking straps on the rudder, and the starboard one which was never used was stowed on deck in the wheelbox. The paint was dry by half past four, so I told Bill he could re-stow the kicking strap. The cabin scuttle joined the wheelbox on the port side and a narrow seat went the length of the box on the starboard side. When he re-stowed the chain, Bill evidently woke the Skipper from his afternoon nap. I was sitting down when the Old Man came on deck. He looked at the kicking strap which was about one foot out of its usual position, and immediately hit me alongside the jaw with his clenched fist saying, "What do you mean by stowing that there?" This was too much, and I retaliated, knocking his hat over the side. He swore and said "Get in the boat and pick that hat up." I got in the boat, poked his hat under with an oar, and rowed ashore. I was in my working gear and had no money, but stayed ashore until midnight. I then rowed back and went down the focsle unmolested.

No mention was made of this incident the next day. It rankled on both sides, but the next episode was even worse. Three days later we were becalmed and at anchor off Beachy Head, holding her against the west going tide. A light breeze sprang up, and he gave the order "Up anchor." When the anchor was up I unshipped my handle and dropped it rather heavily to the deck. He immediately punched me on the nose drawing blood, and said, "I will teach you to knock my ship about." I had had enough, I was reaching my full strength, and he was beyond his prime. I put my arms around him, my chin on his chest and flattened him backwards on the deck. I then placed my heavy boot on this throat and told him he was behaving like a madman, and unless he promised to behave, I would crush his throat. He gave in and we proceeded up channel.

When we got to London, Bill packed up. He had seen enough of the *Glenmore* and her Skipper. Brooks could not get another Mate to sail with him and he still dominated me enough to crush any ideas of leaving. I had nowhere to go anyhow. He shipped his nephew—a big raw boned bricklayer's labourer—as Third Hand not for his ability, but I believe for his protection.

In June 1925 we loaded a cargo of maize from a wharf above London Bridge, destination Plymouth. The Skipper went to the City, and when he came back, we were nearly loaded and he found that the cargo was literally alive with weevil. There were three weevil to every grain of maize. Within twelve hours the cabin panel work was black with them, also the focsle. They got in the cabin clock and stopped it and even in the barometer. Our food was smothered with the filthy things. Brooks first demanded that the cargo be unloaded, but finally agreed to take it to Plymouth for double freight. We put a few tinned stores into the boat, a kettle teapot, and primus stove and lived in discomfort in the boat until the cargo was delivered. Our fame had gone before us, because we were not allowed into Millbay Dock, but had to discharge on some waste ground outside. We had loaded 137 tons and weighed out 129 tons. I still maintain that eight tons of the cargo

Mate of the Glenmore

walked or flew over the side. We were fumigated out at Plymouth, but it had little effect. We then proceeded to Portland and loaded stone for London. When we took the hatches off in London, the white Portland stone was black with weevil. There was trouble over this and we went on the slipway. A hole was bored in the *Glenmore's* bottom, and she was flushed out from stem to stern with a powerful fire hose. The PLA then took over and sprayed her out with some potent mixture. But we still had weevils. We could no longer carry grain cargoes, and went into the continental brick trade, loading cargoes of French and Belgian bricks for Horse Shoe Jetty, Dagenham. Nearly all of Dagenham and surrounding towns are built with foreign bricks. There were several barges in this trade, including the boomie *Zenobia,* Captain Jesse Farthing, now Skipper of one of Everard's motor ships. Brooks was beginning to fail, but was just as irascible as ever. He was beginning to rely on me more and told me if I stopped with him I would in time take his place as Master of the *Glenmore.*

In March 1925, while sailing up the Thames, we passed a huge steel barge with white sails undergoing trials. She flew a burgee from her topmast head marked *'Will Everard'.* Neither myself nor Brooks thought it within the realms of chance that the 'Useless Dummy' standing alongside him (that was me) would be her proud captain within seven years. She was the largest barge ever built, and looked a picture.

One passage from Calais it blew practically a full gale from the SSE. I had persuaded the Old Man to sail against his better judgement. We scuttled across the channel under foresail, and half mainsail with plenty of water coming on board. About half channel over we had the appearance of a half tide rock, when we saw a full rigged ship carrying a full press of canvas approaching athwart our course. He passed fairly close to us as dry as a bone and doing what I estimated to be sixteen knots. A beautiful picture and a memory that later generations will never know.

There were many other sea going barges that I have not mentioned at this time, commanded by such men as 'Scamper' who was thirty years in one ship (Covenden's *Thistle*), Jimmy Martin, Bert and Dick Strange, Ketley—real seamen and sea going bargemen, not the hedge hoppers that plied their cargoes in the Thames Estuary.

SAILORMAN

I would like to pay a tribute to the Missions to Seamen and some of the good people who work for them. I had been fortunate in going to sea with a captain who — as I have mentioned before — was morally decent and fairly abstemious. During the time I was under him he also did his best to choose my company for me — a thing that was not at the time appreciated. Being to all intents and purposes homeless, it was a pleasure and privilege to be able to use the Missions to Seamen's Hostels in the various ports. Seamen are notoriously wild, although not so much now as in the 1920s and for centuries before that. There are various reasons for this improvement: general education, pictures, wireless and, not least, the better accommodation on ships, and fixed hours of duty. For the great majority it used to be "Work hard and play hard." For the lonely seamen the Flying Angel Hostels used to, and still do, make a welcome haven: that is, if he is looking for decent company and relaxation. While I was Third Hand of the *Glenmore,* my small wage did not go very far and I have had many acceptable gifts of warm socks, jerseys, mufflers and even trousers from the Mission. The hostels are in charge of decent God fearing men, who without jamming religion down one's throat, endeavour to minister to the sailors' spiritual and material needs.

Two men in this connection whom I would like to mention are Mr Noble, at that time in charge at Newhaven, and Mr William Coryton. I only met the latter gentleman once but he left a lasting impression on my mind. A lay preacher, he was big in every way. If he had been ordained I feel sure he would have filled a church anywhere. Mr Noble used to make us lads very welcome and if, as sometimes was the case, a large fleet was in, would organize social evenings so that the lads could talk and mix with decent girls. His wife also was a very nice woman who co-operated with him whole-heartedly. I suppose bargemen and sailors are no worse than others in this respect but the great majority fail to appreciate the good work done by the Mission and only regard the hostels as a place where they can get something for nothing.

Shrubsall of Greenwich built and owned some fine barges including the *Velonia* and *Vicunia.* The *Velonia* was the only sprittie I remember with a fixed jibboom or bowsprit. I remember Phil Brooks, then of the *Venta,* saying "One of these days I'm going to be Skipper of that one with the horn out." He did later.

Mate of the Glenmore

The *Vicunia* was a fine wooden barge, of 180 tons to her Plimsoll, that later had an unfortunate end. In 1937 when owned by Sully and in charge of the 'Charlie Cricks' she was in collision and sank with a cargo of grain in Yarmouth Harbour. After a period of submersion, she was refloated and fitted with an auxiliary engine. She was also renamed to become the *Orcades*. She was only under way for a period of months when with a cargo of straw from Colchester to Ridham Dock she caught fire, rapidly burnt to the waters edge and sank.

Another barge with an interesting career was the *Ivo* built by Jimmy Little and named after his son, Lieutenant Ivo Little RNAS, who was later killed in the *R38* airship disaster over Hull. I cannot personally vouch for it but Navvy told me that during the 1914-18 war her Skipper sailed her on top of Boulogne breakwater. The crew abandoned her. She later refloated herself and sailed down channel. Reported a 'menace to navigation' she was disposed of by the Navy, to come drifting into Portland Harbour the next day, still unmanned. About 1926 she capsized off the Isle of Wight but lived to do more freights.

Life was not just one succession of gales. There were good times on shore and always new sights and faces. I always regard Devon as the most beautiful county of England and among others the view as one rounds the Mewstone to enter Dartmouth with the small St Petrox Castle nestled against the foot of the shining pink and grey cliffs, is unequalled.

I became acquainted with curiously named anchorages where a barge could ride in safety with the wind from various directions: 'The Park' to the east of Selsey Bill; 'Ryde Roads' and 'Stokes Bay'; 'Jack in the Basket' off Lyminton; and 'Old Harry' to the SE of Poole Bar. At one time we were windbound in Stokes Bay bound up channel with our usual Portland stone. George the Mate had just returned from the shore in the small boat which he had used to get stores. He and his father were going through the bill and I was on the fore deck chopping wood. Two destroyers had been chasing round practising firing torpedoes. One of these apparently became uncontrollable. I had been watching these interesting manoeuvres while engaged in my wood chopping and saw this torpedo bounce out of the water like a huge porpoise. It did this three times and then travelling at great speed headed for the *Glenmore*. I called aft "Is that a torpedo coming for us,

SAILORMAN

Sir?" Navvy took one look and quickly scrambled into the boat followed by George. Neither of them were apparently concerned with my fate. An interesting performance now took place. Navvy had seized an oar and was making a frenzied effort to scull clear of the barge. George had only got his toes hooked under the gunnel of the boat and was hanging on the port taffrail with both hands. It was fortunate for both of them that this was so for the torpedo came straight along the port side of the barge, missing us by about eighteen inches. It then swung round and crashed into Stokes Bay pier. The destroyer steamed up and from her bridge her commander shouted through a megaphone "That was a near one, Old Skipper." The reply of the Old Skipper about "Blankety bits of boys in charge of bankety devils' inventions which they. . . . .knew nothing about," was a joy to hear.

When proceeding to the west of the Isle of Wight Old Harry was the next anchorage; this is a large cylindrical chalk rock detached from the coast and quite prominent. It was 'Harry and his Mother' at one time but the lady has washed away. This is a good roadstead with the wind as far southerly as S by W but if it came to the E of S you are embayed and cannot get out. The only other alternative if you can get your anchors is to take the bar and run into Poole harbour. Captain George Wynn, former Master of the *Alaric* had bought a boomie, the *Dianna*, and had his two sons as crew. The elder, known to all as 'Spider', was Mate. The *Dianna* was lost in this anchorage about 1925.

One of the weapons of my Skipper was heavy sarcasm. When I was first taught to steer, he would watch the twists in the white water of the wake and then say "I don't mind you writing your name in the water, boy, but don't go back and dot the 'i's;" or else "Get hold of the wheel boy. I will rig up a line and spinner to catch some mackerel, you can never catch them on a straight course." Once he left me at the wheel with a fresh NE wind bound west and went below for a nap. When he returned on deck we were well across the West Bay. He peered at the compass and then said "Have you ever been to Torquay boy?" When I innocently replied "Yes Sir," he shouted "Well keep her away a couple of points you are not bound there now." Incidentally, our destination was Plymouth.

I never saw him have a pilot at any of the various ports we went to. He was a stickler for saving expense and the assistance of a tug or motorboat in narrow rivers never entered his head. He would sail the *Glenmore* to a standstill and then, if it was fine, we poked her along with setting booms. If there was too much water for this practice, the Mate and Third Hand wore blisters on their hands and sterns towing the barge by means of rowing the small boat. The Skipper had the busy job of occasionally turning the wheel and shouting "Keep steerage way on her." If there was any wind and it was foul, we used to run a 100 fathom two inch cotton line out, make it fast to some fixed object on the bank and heave her ahead on the mast case winch; or else worst of all, kedge her. This meant letting go the main anchor, rowing a kedge anchor, to which the cotton line had been made fast, to the full extent of the line. Then throwing the kedge over the side of the boat returning on board and taking the weight on the line on the winch. Then we would heave the main anchor off the ground, heave ahead until the line was short, down main anchor. This manoeuvre was repeated until we reached our destination.

We once sailed from Totnes up the River Dart to a village called Tuckeney to load a cargo of cider. The wind died away and it grew dark. It was most eerie with the noise of owls, herons and other birds on the wooded hillsides. We poked and pushed and hove, with leaves and small branches of trees falling to the deck as they were dislodged by the rigging from overhanging trees — but we got there. The *Glenmore* was too large for proper sweeps but at times in an endeavour to get into an anchorage in a calm he would rig two fourteen foot oars through the bight of a line at the main shrouds and make us row.

While I was Mate of the *Glenmore*, I had two experiences of going over the side. The first time at Poole, Dorset, and later at Portsmouth and both while we were moored along side a quay. Like all other spritties the *Glenmore* had a top up bowsprit which was hove up practically vertical when in harbour. When down and in a sailing position the bobstay was hove taught, shrouds taken in and footropes made fast. The footropes were of $2\frac{3}{4}$ inch tarred hemp, with knots spaced regularly at every three feet to prevent slipping. These footropes led from the outer end of the bowsprit into the ship's rail forward and were the only means of getting out onto the bowsprit to stow the jibs. We had had a wet and dirty passage from London to Poole and the jibs were left unfurled until we were moored. It was still raining but the order was given "Get those jibs stowed and the bowsprit up." The Skipper went below and I told the Third Hand I would give him a shout when I wanted his assistance. I clambered out onto the starboard footrope fully rigged in a large oilskin coat with leather knee boots. Due to the wet, the footropes were bar tight and leading up at a fair angle. I leaned across the top of the bowsprit, caught hold of the guts of the jib with both hands and gave a heave to bring it up onto the spar. As I did this my feet slipped off the footrope and in I went. When I came to the surface my clothes and boots were so loaded with water that I could not even swim the few feet necessary to reach the bobstay. Although the quay had appeared deserted somebody evidently saw me go in, for as I surfaced for the second time, a life belt smacked into the water within arms length and I promptly grabbed it. I was hauled out of the water like a half drowned rat. I changed and finished the job I had set out to do. At tea that evening the Skipper said "What was all the noise on deck this afternoon?" I enlightened him and all he said was "That will teach you."

On the second occasion we were moored at Flathouse Quay, Portsmouth, where there is a rise and fall of about fifteen feet. There was a strong wind straight off the quay and it being high tide the barge was about eight feet from the quayside. After tea I had washed and dressed with the intention of going to the pictures and hove the barge alongside for'ard with a hawse line. I asked the Skipper if he would slack this line up after I had got ashore to allow the barge to fall with the tide. He was in one of his bad moods and told me to slack the line myself and get ashore as best I could seeing that I was so land crazy. As usual when these things happen the rain had made the paintwork wet and slippery. I released the line and the barge started blowing away from the quay. I stepped on to a collar board or bow rail and took a flying leap, missed the quay and went in. I swam to some iron steps embedded in the quay wall and dragged myself onto the quay. In my temper I determined that I would not give in but went to a public urinal, wrung my wet clothes out as well as I could and had three hours of wet and warm in the picture house.

In March 1926, Captain Brooks was ill in Calais but finally managed to get the barge to her destination in London and went home. He never returned on board. George took us back

A news photograph of the 'Will Everard' ashore at Pevensey Bay, 1938

All hands to the mainsheet—the Author, Dick and George Dray, 1936

The wreck of the 'Scotia' at Yarmouth, 6 October 1929

to Woolwich where we lay for two months. Remembering his promise that I would have her when he was finished and finding out that he was unlikely to return, I worked like a nigger—scraped the cabin panel work, burnt all the old paint off inside and out and scraped all the spars. At this time I also rigged and fitted out the *Glendevon* unassisted.

I used to go and see 'Old Brooks' during his illness until he died. The doctors were uncertain of the cause of death and a Post Mortem was held. It was found to be an abscess on the heart. Perhaps that accounted for his tantrums.

Without warning I was informed by Ralph Cunis that a new Skipper and Mate would be on board the *Glenmore* next day to take her to the 'Ballast Engine' to load for up river. What a degradation for the proud *Glenmore*! I was given the option of taking a small river barge called the *Wumps* or working as a labourer on the yard. I chose the latter until I could get a sea going berth. A Mr King was resident manager at the time and he and his wife, hearing of my predicament, very kindly invited me to live with them.

There were naturally other good men and ships at this period which I have not mentioned. One exceptional one was *Goldfinch*, the only barge I ever saw with a square rigged topsail similar to a schooner. Also Goldsmith's large fleet including *Oceanic, Britannic, Maymond* and *Runic*; the boomies *Lord Lansdowne* and *Mazeppa;* the *Ethel Edith, Leading Light* and *Kindly Light*. These two latter I believe are still doing good work in the West Indies. Neither have I mentioned Everard's fleet. I had not come into contact with many of them, but remember the loss of the *Lord Kitchener* between the Start and Dartmouth. The Mate and Cook were drowned and the Skipper, Jimmy Stowe, managed to climb the cliffs in an exhausted condition. When he knocked at the door of a house and asked for succour he was told to go elsewhere. There were also the barges of various firms engaged in the Channel Island stone trade, loading road metal and other types of stone from Alderney, Jersey and Guernsey. This was a dangerous piece of water for sailing craft as the tides run with great violence and there are numerous rocks. There were many casualties in this particular trade. There were also cargoes of boulders, large round stones used for crushing in the cement mills, from Fecamp, and at the other end of the Continental Home Trade, Oyster shells from Zerichzee in Holland and mineral waters from the Rhine.

CHAPTER **4**

Joining Everards

Before commencing my labouring job I visited the 'City' and presented myself to Mr Bert Schooley of the firm of Such and Schooley, Shipbrokers. He had been receiving letters in my handwriting for three years signed G Brooks, seeking freights and other business letters. I explained my predicament and asked if he could get me a berth. He at once said, "Come round with me to Mr Everard." The office we visited was in Great Tower Street. I then saw Mr Will Everard for the first time. Mr Schooley said "If you want a good chap for one of your barges Will, here's one. Six years with old 'Navvy' in the *Glenmore*." Mr Will looked at me quizzically and said "Six years with 'Navvy' Brooks, that is a recommendation in itself." He said "I haven't anything in the barges at the moment, will you go AB in one of my steamships?" To my credit I replied "No thank you Sir, I am a Bargeman." He then said "Where can I get hold of you if I want you?" I was able to give him Cunis's telephone number at Woolwich. I was living on the premises by night and all the office staff knew me if the call came during the day. It came a week later and a voice with which I was to become very familiar said "Will you go Mate on my *Cambria*?" In a disappointed tone I said "Mate—I wanted a Skipper's berth." He then replied "We will see about that later; do you want the job or not?" So I came to Everard's.

I joined next morning at Greenhithe and found that the reason for the vacant berth was the former Mate of the *Cambria* had refused to assist in loading a cargo of bagged cotton cake into his vessel. I had no scruples on this score having hove out thousands of tons of cement. I was introduced to my new Skipper, Charlie Wright, and he said "I am pleased it is you; I thought they would send me some dud." This was rather flattering as I had never seen him before in my life. He was expected to work cargo but had paid a man to do his share. Mr Everard at this period used to take on contracts for which he had not got sufficient sea going craft, load the cargoes into lighters out of the import ships and float them to Greenhithe until he had a ship available. I took charge of the stowing and was pleased to find that the barge put 20 tons more cargo under the hatches then she would have done if loaded by London dockies. We loaded 183 tons under the hatches which we took to the little port of Wells in Norfolk. I found my new Skipper very pleasant to get on with and appreciative of my work. He had not had much more barging experience than myself. He had become Skipper at an early age and had then gone 'Deep Sea' and had only recently resumed his barging career. He had little to teach me apart from how to read a chart, plot a course and take a four point bearing.

Navvy had never used a chart in his life and his method of taking a fix was to lay his hand athwart the compass bowl, wait five minutes and do it again. From this he appeared to get all the information he wanted or else he would estimate the time we shut out the lights of a town astern after passing a headland and then say "Keep her down so and so." I never knew him wrong. He used to work up through the Gore and Four Fathoms Channel in the dark, loaded ship, and I do not remember 'grounding'. It was from Navvy also that I learned how to cheat the tide in rivers and round the coast by working the eddies. In fine settled weather in the Channel he would keep off during the day for the sea breeze and before it fell too light, come right in under the land to catch the hot air coming off during the night in the form of wind.

From Wells we proceeded empty to Antwerp to load coal for Queenborough in the River Swale. It was during the long 1926 coal strike. It was a very poor quality coal and I learnt what self-combustion meant. The cargo heated and by the time we had discharged had burnt a small hole in the ceiling. On board the *Glenmore* I did not know what an 'Owner' was but in Everards found the various Captains very Owner-conscious —and for good reason. There was also more rivalry and chase than I had previously experienced.

I found several other skippers in Everard's firm whom I have

SAILORMAN

previously mentioned in other ships. Jack Josh had been established in the steel *Greenhithe* since 1923. Incidentally during the First World War when he had the *Persevere* he had been taken prisoner by a German destroyer. He told me that he was at anchor off the North Foreland with several other barges when in the night the destroyer came alongside and took them on board. Her commander could speak excellent English and had Josh on the bridge with him crossing the North Sea. He asked what the lights had been inside of the *Persevere* and Jack told him that they were other barges. The commander then said "When you get back to England after the war, tell your friends that they were fortunate. I intended to bombard them thinking they were lights ashore at Ramsgate." There was also Cully, Frank Day and Nobby Finch, all recently newcomers to the firm. The reason for so many new skippers in one firm was that Mr Will was then pioneering with diesel driven motor coasters in keen competition with the Dutch who were rapidly reducing freights on the British coast to an uneconomic level. His long-service skippers were going into these motor vessels as fast as they were commissioned.

The founder of the firm of F T Everard & Sons Limited was Mr Frederick T Everard, Senior. When I first joined the firm he was still hale and hearty and had the reputation of being a gentleman to work for. He had originally been foreman shipwright at Keep's yard at Greenhithe and then started building barges on his own. The four first were the *Britisher, Scotia, Cambria* and *Hibernia,* built in that order.

I now began to get experience on the East Coast which apart from my one trip to Lowestoft was new to me. I found that our principle trade was 'cattle-cake' from London to Wells and Kings Lynn, and coal from the Humber to Margate. Our actual loading port for coal was at a coal-tip situated at Keadby. This is a small village on the north bank of the River Trent. The Trent and the Ouse joining the River Humber just below Blacktoft. There was only a small jetty at Keadby and sometimes there would be a dozen barges at anchor in the river awaiting their turn to load. The river has been improved in recent years by the building of a large training wall at the confluence of the Trent and Ouse. But at this time it was dangerous to lie at anchor on spring tides because of the 'Aeger'. This was a tidal wave similar to the Severn Bore but not on such a grand scale. The tide ebbed for nearly ten hours

58

and then as the flood got over the shallows at Trent mouth a wall of water four feet high would come tearing up the river. We used to have to stand by to pay out more cable as this tide hit us to ease the blow and prevent being swept up the river and athwart the bridge.

I had only been in the *Cambria* a few months when there was another shift around, and we took over the *Scotia*. This was a fine wooden barge of 200 tons, very handy for her size and as stiff as a church. She would put up with all the canvas you liked to put on her whereas the *Cambria*, being flare sided, was a bit tender. She was later practically thrown away and foundered off Yarmouth.

Charlie Wright had neither the sagacity nor the knowledge of the coast that Navvy had possessed. We once bore up and ran right back from the Owers lightship to the Downs when bound for Southampton. There was a strong west wind when he turned despite my remonstrance and pointing out that we could ride in the Park, an anchorage to the east of Selsey Bill, with the wind touching off the land. He was very fair and generous in his praise for a job well done but without a lot of initiative. I had observed that when a fleet of barges got together wind-bound, the skippers would get together and discuss the weather and the prospects. If the wind came right one did not like the look of the stars, another thought the town lights were blinking too much or the wind had veered too quickly. Many a passage was missed in this way. Then some hero would muster and the others follow him like a flock of sheep for good or ill. I determined that if ever I had charge I would be a lone wolf.

The only time I quarelled with Charlie Wright was when we loaded a cargo of oil cake from Dunkirk to Hull. He went ashore before we commenced loading and was still missing two days after we had completed loading. During this time the wind had been moderate southerly, a beautiful wind for the Humber. He finally showed up much the worse for wear and decided to go to sea. Once clear of the harbour he turned in. We got half way across the North Sea when the wind flew into the north-west. I called him on deck and he decided to run back to Dunkirk still leaving me at the wheel. When we got into the North Hinder light, we found the wind was still south on the French coast so round once more until we met the north-west wind again. We turned again and were approaching

SAILORMAN

Dunkirk the next day after I had been at the wheel for fifteen hours when he saw another barge belonging to our firm coming out of Dunkirk. He now wanted to try and make the North Foreland but I refused duty and we quarrelled violently. I decided to write to Mr Everard and remind him that I had asked to come into the firm as a Skipper and was still waiting for the chance. We loaded meal back from Hull to London and upon arrival at Greenhithe I was told to bring my gear ashore and commence rigging out the *John Bailey*.

Old Mr Everard who gave me the berth said "You have got to start at the bottom of the ladder, sonny," to which I said "Yes Sir, thank you." The *John Bailey* had originally been a Margate hoy barge and had just been sheathed. She was only 100 tons burden to sea and would carry 115 tons in the river. I was given brand new rigging and a new set of sails and fitted her out. Her cabin was in a deplorable condition and I spent many night hours during the ensuing weeks fumigating, scrubbing, scraping and painting to make it habitable. Finally in November 1927 I loaded my first cargo as Master. This was a cargo of cement from the Tunnel works at Thurrock to a ship in the Royal Albert Dock. I had as yet little knowledge of the finer points in sailing a barge. As a Mate I had hove down docks on my own responsibility and berthed alongside various wharves but I had yet to learn how far a barge would carry her way under various conditions and quantities of sail. I had stood at the wheel and tacked up various rivers but always at somebody else's direction.

Before sailing from Greenhithe to the Tunnel, 'Knocker' Hart the Skipper of the *Scot*, gave me valuable advice on how to approach the jetty because of the eddy-tide and where to touch the anchor on the ground to let her swing. Knocker was, a well known character on the Thames, a typical cockney and the origin of various humorous yarns which are still bandied about the river. Some have already been told by various authors but as far as I know the following have never appeared in print.

Mr Will ordered him ashore early one morning and said "I want your barge over to the Tunnel to load cement. What is your hold like?" Knocker replied "It's blankety well wet fru and ain't fit to load." Mr Will said "Well, get off there and take your hatches off to let the air through her. See me after breakfast." After breakfast Knocker was again ashore and reported that the hold was still wet. Mr Will who was rather hasty said "Take the big blow lamp off and dry it up. If it isn't dry when I come from London this evening your sacked. Knocker went off and started drying up. He later came ashore for his beer and left the blow lamp burning down the hold. After a good session he returned on board to find a hole burnt in the ceiling and the hold still wet. That evening he waited outside the house for Mr Will and as he stepped out of his car Knocker said "Me hold ain't dry and if you sack me again today, I'll leave."

On another occasion, Knocker who likes his pint, left his boat tied up to the causeway outside the White Hart one evening. He stayed until closing time and then made for the causeway. In the meantime some kids had taken the boat for a row and left her elsewhere. Knocker was muzzy in the fresh air and the night was dark but he knew where he had left his boat. Deceived by a shadow caused by a street lamp he stepped straight into the water. Telling the tale against himself he said "I stepped into me bleeding boat and she wasn't there."

Another favourite haunt of Knocker's in recent years was the Ship and Lobster at Gravesend. Knocker rowed ashore one evening for a convivial drink and to his disgust found he was the only customer. The landlord's dog was in the bar so he started playing with it. His idea of play was to ruffle the dog's ears and then bend down and grimace at it. The dog put up with this treatment for a while, and then, either angry or fascinated by Knocker's rather prominent nose—buried his teeth in it. He had to go to hospital for treatment and next day telling of the incident said "I was only playing with the bleeding tyke and it spoilt me beauty." If he reads this I hope he will not blush and I am always good for a pint.

I later sailed in his company to Yarmouth when I had the *Hibernia*. We met a fresh easterly wind and had a bit of a bang to get to Yarmouth. As well as strong drink, Knocker was also addicted to strong language. Describing the difference in our respective vessels he said to others in a pub "There was Jimmy as snug as a bug in a rug and there was us, seas half way up the bleeding mast."

There are two more stories of Knocker. He was sailing up through Lower Hope reach one dark night with a fair wind. His sails squared off on the starboard side. As he was approaching the Ovens light buoy, his vision to leeward being obscured by the foot of the mainsail. He had to leave the wheel occasionally, walk to the main hawse and peer under the sail to see the flashing light of the buoy. Knocker misjudged and hit the buoy putting the light out. Next morning at Greenhithe he had to see Mr Will and reported that he had hit the buoy and put the light out. Mr Will said "You will have to make out a written report. How did it happen?" Knocker replied in true cockney "Well I looked under the mainsail and the light was going In-Aht, In-Aht, In-Aht, In-Aht. Presently there was a bang and it went aht altogether."

The last story about this particular character occurred when he was Skipper of the *Scot*. He had anchored outside Harwich when a mailboat came out of the harbour, collided with the *Scot* and sank her. Knocker and his Mate had time to pick up their more personal possessions before taking to the small boat. They were promptly picked up and taken back to Harwich. Knocker 'phoned Mr Will to impart the news. When connected, his first words were "We're dahn the pond!" Mr Will said, "What do you mean? Down the Pond?" and Knocker replied, "A mailboat hit us off Harwich; we're sunk and me gold watch wiv it." The latter remark no doubt having a bearing on making a claim for lost gear.

A couple of incidents are worth recalling of another old timer, Captain Frank 'Cully' Teovil, the Master of the *Britisher*. He had been asked to join the firm by the founder Mr F T Everard and his first ship in Everards was the boomie *Evelyn*. Cully was a very careful and cautious Skipper, who did less freights than any other Master in the firm. I never knew him do any damage but with his caution was often the butt of Mr Will's sarcasm. In January 1930 five of us Masters were in the outer office at Great Tower Street awaiting orders. Mr Will came out from the inner sanctum and said "I have got a cargo for you, Cully. 170 tons of cotton cake for Poole. Proceed to the Millwall Dock next tide." Cully said "Thank you, Mr Will." Whereupon Mr Will said "There is only one snag—they want the cargo there this year."

Cully had two telegrams hung up in his cabin. By some miracle he had beaten Bradley's *Lord Haig* to Yarmouth with a cargo of cement. He sent a telegram to London "ARRIVED YARMOUTH BEAT LORD HAIG". The reply telegram came the same day and consisted of one word "HOORAY". On the second occasion, Cully had discharged a cargo of wheat at Shoreham and was ordered to Cantly to load a cargo of sugar. After a lapse of two weeks with no move from Cully, his orders were altered and he was told to proceed to Calais, for a cargo of stone. A further week elapsed when Cully decided that the conditions were right for sailing, so he sent a telegram "BRITISHER SAILING HIGH WATER". Before high tide the answer had arrived, consisting of the two words "ABOUT TIME". If possible Cully would avoid the usual drinking sessions with other skippers on arrival in harbour but would slip away on his own. What his assignments were, I do not know but if seen going ashore and asked where he was off to, he would cryptically reply, "Old rats like cheese." I think the fact that he had been asked to come into the firm, instead of seeking employment, was the only reason he lasted so long.

Another character who I have only casually mentioned was 'Scamper', who took charge of Covenden's *Thistle* when she was new and stayed in her for thirty years. When buying stores he would get butchers puzzled by asking for the 'front part of a land surveyor' when he wanted a bullock's head or 'underground mutton' when we wanted rabbits.

I loaded four or five river cargoes and on 1 January 1928 loaded 100 tons of oil cake from London to Dover. At this time Mr Everard was giving young chaps the chance to make good in the barges. Some did and some failed. A great deal to do with this was if you were lucky enough to avoid trouble until you had gained confidence in yourself and experience as Master. I was one of the fortunate ones and for the first years could do little wrong. That particular passage to Dover I left Goldsmith's 240 ton *Oceanic* and Covenden's 160 ton *Thistle* at anchor in the Swatchway off Yantlet and with a SW gale proceeded with my 100 tons of cake. As I approached Margate the wind veered to the NW and I had a fair wind all the way. We sailed empty for London and loaded wheat for Dover. I made another quick passage—and here is where luck comes in—avoided a NW gale by a fluke on the return passage in the following way. We used to have a motor boat tow us from the dock at Dover to the outer harbour. We finished discharging just before dark and I wanted to proceed to sea at once. The motor boat had broken down and I could not get out of the dock. That night it blew a full gale from the NNW. It moderated by dawn and I towed out clear. As we were sailing from the harbour we met the S/B *Madrali* in tow, she had been dismasted during the night, a thing which could equally well have happened to me.

After this cargo we arrrived at Greenhithe at 8 am on a Saturday morning. I was told to proceed up river to Silvertown to load sugar for Sandwich. We were alongside at noon loaded in three hours and back at Greenhithe by 6 in the evening. I had not signed 'Bills of Lading' and only knew that I was for Sandwich. There was a southerly gale and we anchored off Greenhithe. At 3 am on the Sunday morning I felt the vessel heel over and went on deck to investigate. The wind had veered to the NW so we scrambled under way. I was moored at Sandwich by 5 pm. We arrived twenty four hours before the Bill of Lading and the notification that we were sailing. That month as well as the three cargoes previously mentioned, I loaded and discharged a river cargo. I was beginning to make a name for myself. In March 1928 Mr Will asked me if I would like to take the *Royalty*, later lost at Dunkirk in 1940. I refused and, when asked for my reasons, replied "I don't want to go up in the firm like a rocket and come down just as fast." He said "You won't come down if you are any good; but perhaps you are wise, I don't want to hurry you along."

I refer frequently to Mr Will because he was the member of the family we were most in contact with. The directors of the firm were old Mr Everard, his wife, Mr Fred, Mr Will, Miss Ethel and Mr Alf. The old couple lived in a large recently built house known as The Warren opposite our shipyard. Here all decisions affecting the firm were made. The fleet of sea going barges then consisted of the four new steel barges of 280 tons, the *Will, Alf, Fred* and *Ethel Everard*—they were launched in that order—the *Scotia, Cambria, Hibernia, Britisher, Martha, Royalty, Mary Graham, Lady Mary, Lady Maud* and the boomie *Martinet* and various river barges.

Freddie Bridger had the *Will*. He was a hard bitten old man who went to sea in practically any weather without thought of consequence. One story of him was that he was running up Channel when Skipper of the boomie *Evelyn* and the Mate called him on deck. It was Freddie's watch below. The Mate was having difficulty in keeping her straight with a strong following wind and suggested that the mainsail be reefed down. Freddie said "She's alright boy. The moon will be up presently and eat the wind." An hour later there was a violent bang and the guts of the mainsail blew out. Freddie dashed on deck and said "What have you done to that sail?" The Mate, disgruntled, replied "The bloody moon has eaten it up."

I once saw him in an amusing incident. Practically the whole of the fleet were wind bound at Yarmouth laden with sugar beet from Cantly. Mr Will wanted them at sea and had ordered all the skippers to be in the brokers office at 9 am on Sunday morning. We all collected at 8.30 am swapping yarns and smoking so that by 9 am the general office of T Small Co Shipbrokers, looked like a public bar with matches and tobacco ash scattered all over it. Billie Stuart the shipping clerk then put the phone call through. Mr Will immediately asked for Bridger to be put on. Freddie held the receiver at arms length offering it round with an imploring look on his face. He had not the sense to clap his hand over the receiver but said loudly "Who wants this bloody thing. I don't want to speak to him."

Jimmy Mole skippered the *Alf*. I knew little about him at the time but we became firm friends and in my opinion he was the best and smartest bargeman of our new generation. Josh now had the *Fred* and Bert Wadhams the *Ethel*. I first knew him when, as Mate of the *Lord Haig* he was knocked unconscious off the South Foreland by a cringle that flew out of the jib sheet when tacking. Wright still had the *Scotia,* Cully the *Britisher* and Nobby Finch the *Cambria*. He had won both the Thames and Medway race the previous year, 1927, the first race since before the 1914-18 war. 'Dick the Dagger' had the *Royalty*. When I asked him how he had acquired his unusual nickname, he told me that when he was a boy an old Skipper said "That boy is as sharp as a dagger," and it is Dick the Dagger to this day. Old Dick Lutchford had the *Lady Mary*, Jack King had the *Greenhithe,* Bob Pringle the *Lady Maud*. Frank Ellis a chap about my age had the *Mary Graham*, we were to have many a keen sail against each other later. Tommy Willis had the *Hibernia*; he later had to abandon the *Ethel Everard* at Dunkirk in 1940, to his everlasting regret. Tommy is still a bargeman at heart although he has been in power for many years.

I never slept in my bunk once during the eight months I had the *John Bayley*. I took my responsibility too heavily. I was confined to river work from February till June and hated it. I then tackled Mr Will about a ship saying that I wanted to go

SAILORMAN

to sea again and that if not as Skipper, I would go back Mate
for the privilege of getting to sea. He lectured me and said I
needed river experience and must stop where I was.

In June I took part in my first barge race nominally as Master
of the *John Bayley*. In reality she was sailed by old Tom Coker
a Master of long standing in the firm. I rather resented this
arrangement at the time but was still learning and found that
barge racing was an art distinct from sailing a barge. That
year the barges raced, although the big J class yachts cancelled their race from Southend because there was too much
wind. The first barge rounded the half way mark, the Mouse
lightship, in two hours three minutes and all the barges were
round in under the two hours fifteen minutes. The course was
from the Lower Hope round the Mouse and back to
Gravesend. These races were hard work but good fun and
allowed the bargeman to show their skill and courage. I subsequently took part in every barge race until 1938. The only
exception was 1929 when old Mr Everard died two days before
the race. The firm withdrew their entries and all white paint
on board the ships was painted blue as a token of mourning
and respect. He was a fine old gentleman and a restraining in-
fluence on Mr Will.

A month later July 1928 I was walking along the village high
street with Cully when Mr Will burst out of Accuba House
and called me over. He then said "We are putting you in the
Hibernia, will that satisfy you?" Naturally I was proud and
pleased although the appointment caused a certain amount of
heart burning in the firm. I thanked him and he said "Right,
it will be in about a fortnight," and went back into the house.

66

CHAPTER 5

Skipper of Hibernia

The *Hibernia* was a fine wooden coaster of 180 tons burden and the finest sea ship I have ever sailed in. She was fast and in a seaway with half a gale of wind you could trim your sheets slack the foresail to the mast and she would sail herself. I took over the *Hibernia* at Keadby when she arrived empty. My good luck continued. We loaded the same day and within forty two hours we were at Margate, a distance of 230 miles. As an example of luck, a large tanker had gone ashore on the Haisborough Sands a week earlier and broken in half. One half sunk off Cromer. A conical wreck buoy was established the seaward side of this position which was only just beneath the surface at low tide. On that passage I was off Cromer in poor visibility at dawn and passed inside the buoy instead of outside. I could easily have lost my new ship.

At this period I was doing a considerable amount of damage not so much due to lack of experience but to taking too many chances. Mr Will confided to a senior Master that he did not know what to do about that chap in the *Hibernia*; "he does more freights than anybody and twice as much damage."

In December 1928, *Lady Daphne* bound light from Weymouth to one of the clay ports, was caught in an easterly blizzard, approaching Start Point. Her Skipper, Buck Whitby, went forward to attend to something and disappeared over the side. The Mate, Ken Mann, who later lost his life by magnetic mine in the last war, sent up flares. The Mate and Third Hand were taken out by the Plymouth lifeboatmen and the ship was abandoned. She sailed down channel herself and finding the only sandy piece of beach among the rocks of the

67

SAILORMAN

Scilly Isles, beached herself and rolled onto her side. George Barker later went to the Isles, righted her and sailed her back to Rochester practically undamaged.

The *Lady Daphne* and *Lady Jean* had the distinction of having a medallion on them "Built by Short Bros" (of seaplane and flying boat fame). When they were extending their aeroplane factory, they took over what used to be Jimmy Little's yard as a going concern. They also finished the partly built *Lord Haig*. The *Lord Haig,* after her first trial with a river cargo of coal, made so much water that she had to be put ashore. Her seams were then caulked with brown paper until they took up. This method was used so that the paper could spew out and leave a fair seam. She was never very tight and was lost off the Humber in about 1928, Master Jack Gladstone—Gentleman Jack.

In January 1929 the *Hibernia* needed two inwales and several new timbers. As these repairs were going to take some weeks, I was asked to fit out the *Royalty*. This I did and in company with the *Cambria* loaded a cargo of rice meal from Tilbury Dock to Hull. That is a voyage that will live in my memory for ever. My elder stepbrother had just finished a period of service in the RAF and was at a loose end. I suggested that he come for a trip with me, which he did. We sailed on 10 February 1929 and anchored off Yantlet for two days with fog and light NE winds. At midday on the 12 the wind came away from the SW and Nobby in the *Cambria* suggested mustering and trying to get as far as Harwich. I knew that the *Cambria* was faster than the *Royalty* and asked Nobby not to run away from us. He agreed and we set sail.

The *Royalty* was very slow and as straight as a plank, having no sheer whatever. The *Cambria* kept company with us for the first hour and then to save his water and daylight through the Wallet Spitway, Nobby woke her up and was soon out of sight. By the time I was abreast of the Spitway, which at that time was not marked with a light buoy, it was dark and four hours ebb. The lights of Clacton were not visible to get a bearing so I decided to keep running down the Swin outside the Gunfleet. The wind fell light from the NW and we were enveloped in dense fog. We crawled away down sailing and sounding until 4 am when I let go the anchor in six fathoms being doubtful of my position. The fog cleared at noon with a nice breeze from the ENE. I found we were abreast of Orfordness and fairly

68

close in. We got under way and headed north. Within two hours there was a full gale from the ESE. It was bitterly cold and by the time we were abreast of Lowestoft it was again dark with a nasty sea. I said "We have got two alternatives: either anchor under the lee of the Scroby and chance having to be taken out of her; or keep running."

We decided on the latter. By the time we were off Cromer the topsail had blown to ribbons and we were running under jib foresail and half mainsail. The seas were tremendous and as we were not fast enough to keep ahead of them we were pooped continually. The seas were mountainous and as the water fell on board it froze. It took two men to steer her and one continuously kept a lookout aft to give warning of those seas which looked like breaking on board. The compass was situated in such a position that it could not be seen with the hood on. I had removed the hood and as the water broke over the top of the wheelhouse it landed on the compass and turned it at all angles. The boat had already been washed out of the davits and had disappeared. We could only try and keep her stern to sea with the sails gybed on the land. Visibility was poor as it always is when you get a real smokey easterly gale. I caught a glimpse of a lightship about 2 pm and being doubtful whether it was the Dudgeon or the Inner Dowsing, decided to gybe and run in to pick up the land. We made a landfall at Mablethorpe and had to gybe on again. This meant somebody unhooking the weather running backstay and hooking the other one up as she gybed. I had not the heart to order anybody else along the deck so did it myself. While doing so I was washed out straight several times and only prevented myself being washed over the side by clinging desperately to the rigging.

During all this period the cook had been locked down the cabin. The water began to freeze inside my kneeboots so I nipped below to get some dry boot stockings. I found the cook on the cabin floor with my two pillows over the top of his head to drown the noise. I roused him into pulling my boots off and rubbing my feet with a coarse towel. I am sure this was the only thing that prevented me from being frostbitten. Wet through otherwise but dryly shod, I returned to the deck feeling better.

I had gone so far into the land to fix my position that I now found myself to leeward in the broken water on Rosse Spit.

While in this broken water the *Royalty* buried her head to the main mast and another huge sea curled on board from the weather bow. She shuddered and I thought she would never come up. She did eventually minus the foresail which had carried away with the weight of the water. As she freed herself I was amazed to see the foscle scuttle hatch complete with flushing board on the main hatches. It had been padlocked but washed off as a whole. I dashed forward and managed to get it on again. The shrouds and deadeyes on either side were one solid block of ice six feet long and about as high. There was not a running rope on board that was not as thick as my forearm with ice. We finally made the Humber and anchored inside the Burcome shoal. Every loose article on board had gone including the ventilation cowl, the galley funnel and the cabin funnel. After anchoring I made a deck funnel out of a canvas backed chart and we got the cabin fire going. We rubbed ourselves down, donned the nearest thing we could find to dry clothes and then blocked the draughts out of the cabin and got a real fug up. Also a damned good meal of eggs and bacon and hot tea.

When we arrived at Hull we were directed into what proved a bad berth and the *Royalty* pushed her plank ends past the transom and lifted the wheel house off the deck. She was already making water due to her punishing passage but this increased the leaking. I had a busy time going to solicitors to make statements and to a public notary to swear an oath as to the nature of the passage and arranging for a boat and sails and so forth to be sent to Hull. The *Cambria* was still in Harwich. Mr Everard decided that as she was leaking I had better bring her back to London empty. I sailed by the share and there was no taste in nothing. Incensed about this and the running about on shore I was having, I wrote a pretty hot letter to him giving him my views. The next day we sailed from Greenhithe. The wind was now ENE moderate but still bitterly cold. There were still half a dozen loaded barges in Grimsby Roads bound south but I was determined to get the trip over and get out of the noble *Royalty*.

We proceeded to sea and could not quite fetch round Cromer. I had to stand off head to sea for a couple of hours which gave her another good hammering, she now being light. I arrived at Greenhithe at 8 the following evening and made her fast on the coal wharf where she visibly started to settle down. I went

The formidable George 'Navvy' Brooks/Jack Nunn junior

Jimmy Mole in 1970/George Dray, Mate of the 'Will', 1936

Dick the Dagger in 1950/Jesse Farthing in 1974

Frank 'Cully' Toevil/Nobby Finch

ashore and knocked on the door of Accuba house, Mr Will's residence, to report. A maid answered the door and announced who I was. Mr Will came charging down the hall in his shirtsleeves with the greeting "I am going to pull your bally nose for you—that letter! We don't allow employees to write like that to us." I stood my ground and after he had got it all off his chest he said "Don't you sleep on that *Hibernia* tonight, you might catch a chill." Very thoughtful but any chill I would catch on the *Hibernia* was nothing like the *cold* I had caught on my trip in the *Royalty*. Our stormy voyage frightened my Mate and Third Hand off the sea for life. They both left and never went to sea again. The Mate later had charge of the only commercial sailing Norfolk wherry in existence.

My *Hibernia* was now ready and we did several cargoes. There was a lot of friendly rivalry among the Skippers when bound for the same port and not so friendly if they were of another firm and had to be beaten for turn to discharge. Frank Ellis now had the *Greenhithe* and although we were good pals, we used to sail hard against each other. At one time we had both loaded sugar from Cantly to London and he challenged me to sail to London for the price of a new hat. He was bound to Butler's Wharf and I to St Katherines dock on the opposite side of the river, just below Tower Bridge. I beat him by an hour but in doing so blew my foresail away. We had drinks in the Queens Head next day when I collected my winnings and pulled his leg. We were both ordered back to Cantly for another cargo and I explained that I would have to stop at Greenhithe next morning to get another foresail and main hatch tarpaulin. Frank heard me making these arrangements and as we parted company near Tower Bridge to go to our respective ships, he let me cross the road and then shouted "See you at Yarmouth, if you are there in time." This was the wrong type of remark to make to Uglow. I went to the nearest telephone and explained to Greenhithe that I would be off there about 1 am and requested that they have a foresail and tarpaulin placed off afloat on the coal barge where I could collect. They agreed and I went on board.

I came out of the dock at 10 pm with a fresh wind WSW. We only had to make one tack in Limehouse Reach and then had a fair wind down the river. I could see the loom of the *Greenhithe* under way ahead of me. By the time we got to

71

Erith, we were close on him and my Mate said "Let us set the mizen Skipper, we can pass him." I explained that I did not want to pass him and that they were to swing their davits out ready to hoist the boat. I then said "I will be on his heel when we get to Greenhithe. I will then shoot up head to wind and shout at the top of my voice, "Let go your anchor." That will be the signal for you two to jump in the boat and get that gear from the coal barge as quickly as possible." This was done, Frankie saw me head up and thought I had anchored. I jilled across the river and back, picked my boat up and proceeded under reduced canvas. When we got to the Lower Hope I could see the *Greenhithe* at anchor with his riding light up and remarked "There he is sound asleep." We then cracked on and were at Cantly next afternoon.

The wind came from the norrard and we loaded and proceeded to sea next day. We passed the *Greenhithe* coming to Yarmouth off Lowestoft. As we passed I stuck my thumb in the air and Frank shook his fist. The governor asked him to explain how the *Hibernia* had done one round him and Frank said "By a dirty trick." Mr Will asked for an explanation and when I told him he laughed and said "They were brought up in the wrong school Jimmy."

After Mr Everard died I found myself at Keadby in company with Nobby in the *Cambria*. I had sailed right up to Keadby where the *Cambria* was loading. One ship was not enough for Nobby and he shouted "Drop your foresail bring her round and let go your anchor." This annoyed me intensely and started a feud that was to last for two years. We both sailed on the same tide bound for Margate. The *Cambria* had been breamed off and blackleaded ready for the barge race whereas the *Hibernia* had not been on the blocks for fourteen months. We had a glorious sail, neck and neck, and finally beat me into Margate by twenty minutes. When we got on shore I said "If my old girl had been cleaned up she would have given you a shaking Nobby." He replied "Don't talk so damned silly, I was only playing with you." I determined he would never play with me again.

He next loaded cement for Southampton and was ordered to tow behind one of our steamers. By the time they got off Margate it was blowing a southerly gale so Nobby slipped his tow rope and went in under the land at Margate. That day I had a similar order only my cargo was for Poole. By the time my ship got to the Foreland the wind had veered WNW and moderated and he towed me to my destination. I loaded clay back to London and then did a sugar cargo from Cantly before Nobby got to Southampton. It gave me great satisfaction when Mr Will was heard to remark "I've paid one man a cheque for £60 and the other one is nearly that amount in debt."

During this feud several of us came out of Yarmouth sugar laden for London including the *Alf, Fred, Ethel* and *Cambria.* There was a fresh wind W by S and I held my stretch and fetched the Shipwash light. The others all stood in to the land. By then it was high water and time for the evening weather forecast. It proved to be wind backing SW or S, all coasts. As the ebb came away the others anchored inside the Whiting bank. I decided to keep going outside the Kentish Knock in an endeavour to fetch the North Foreland. I fetched the North Goodwin lightship, the wind then backed SSW. The others were dead to leeward while I went tearing up along the Kentish land in smooth water with a foot of sheet off. I beat them all by twenty-four hours and was discharged when they arrived. This move did not increase my popularity with some members of the firm.

The *Hibernia* and *Cambria* were sister ships built at Greenhithe. The first Mr F T Everard put his two elder sons, both time served shipwrights, to build them in friendly rivalry. Mr Fred had charge of building the *Hibernia* and Mr Will the *Cambria.* They cost approximately £1900 each and the *Hibernia* carried 5 tons more cargo. One curious fact about the *Hibernia,* I found, was that when running with a strong quartering wind, she would drop her starboard jaw or bow with the sails on the starboard side, much more than the port bow did under similar conditions with the sails on the port side. I mentioned this to Mr Fred at a later date. He smiled and said "When you get back on board take a good look, you will find that she has one less deck plank on the starboard bow than the port side." Presumably nobody had observed this odd fact before.

I soon realised what a fine sea ship the *Hibernia* was, she was flare sided and in a breeze of wind would press down so far and no farther. I now skippered Jerry, the ex-Mate and Master of the *Portland May* as Mate. He did not reign long. In November 1929 we discharged a cargo of oil cake at Poole

SAILORMAN

and had orders to proceed empty to Cantly. There was a lovely fair wind from the WNW but I could not get Jerry out of the pub. He refused to sail until next day. I phoned the governor and asked him to send me another Mate. He had nobody available and suggested that when I could get him on board, I was to proceed to Yarmouth and discharge him there. The following day we sailed. The wind had backed to the SW and was freshening. I knew if we were inside the Isle of Wight it would mean anchoring so held my luff out round St Catherine's Point. The wind continued to back until it was south and blowing a full gale. That night I saw the *Hibernia* put a sea across her main hatch, empty ship, the first and only time. This was just below Beachy Head.

At Dungeness the wire topsail halliard broke and the head of the topsail came down with a run. Even so we were at the North Foreland in nineteen hours from Poole Quay. I had picked a red headed waif up at Poole who had been sleeping rough for a month. He claimed to have no parents. Remembering my own start, he had all my sympathy and I gave him the berth of Third Hand. I was worried about the lad that night and staggered forward to see how he was fairing. I found him sitting on the fore hatch quite happy and he said "A fine sailing breeze Capt'n." I liked his guts.

At daybreak next day I hauled in under the land and proceeded up through the Gore as there was too much sea to go out round the Knock. The inconsistent Jerry went aloft without demur and spliced in new topsail halliards while sitting on the mast head. I sacked him at Yarmouth and my red headed urchin also disappeared but left a souvenir of his voyage in the form of lice. The only time I had seen them. I had to throw away two sets of underwear.

My next Mate was George Dray, a chap a year my junior. He proved the finest Mate a Skipper could have, clean, capable and willing. Nothing was too much trouble for him and he was just as eager to get on with the job as I was. We were shipmates for seven years and became firm friends. It was a pity that when he later went Master, he did not prove the unqualified success he should have been. His health was probably something to do with it for while Mate of the *Hibernia* he contracted a severe attack of pneumonia which left him weak chested.

While Jack King still had the *Greenhithe* and George had not

74

been with me long, we loaded a cargo of asphalt blocks from London to Kings Lynn. The *Greenhithe* was also loaded for Lynn. We needed to keep a fortnight's stores on board in case we had to lay in an open roadstead for any length of time. There were strong NE winds and we anchored off Southend for a week. Then the wind backed to the NW and we both got as far as Yarmouth Roads. There was a further succession of strong N and NE winds and the *Greenhithe* dragged her anchor and had to be assisted into Yarmouth. We continued to ride in the roads with the mizen set smart and pinned in amidships as the drifters do. This kept us bow to wind and sea. We had a week of this and were very short of food. The tug *Tactful* used to come to us every morning and ask if we wanted to be towed in. I used to reply "We are alright but chuck us a few loaves on board."

The Skipper probably thought he could starve us into accepting his aid for he never brought any bread. Finally when reduced to one hambone and four potatoes and the wind easting a couple of points, I decided to try and finish the passage. We got our anchors—we had been riding on two—set the sails smart and headed for the Cockle Gateway. When we left the partial shelter of the Scroby sand and met the open sea, the *Hibernia* jumped practically out of the water and went into the next sea with a 'whoof'. Due to her flare sides she forced the water away from her and I knew we would get our passage. Off the Docking we had our hambone stew. While windbound I had discovered a can of oil under the cabin floor and could not make out what sort it was by smelling it. I decided to put the lip of the can to my mouth. It proved to be lubricating oil and the ship giving a lurch at the wrong moment, I got a good mouthful. The combination of lubricating oil and hambone stew proved too much for my stomach and I was seasick for the first and last time.

My feud with Nobby continued. We would go ashore together and drink and argue and then when we got to sea try and cut each others throats. A dozen of us were windbound in Grimsby Roads bound south: seven of Everards and five of Goldsmiths. We all used to go ashore during the day, the wind was off shore southerly and the vessels were safe, and have a good drink.

One morning the wind had fallen light and there came a little fog draught from the NE. We followed our usual routine and

SAILORMAN

went ashore. After half an hour Nobby said "I have had enough of this, I am going back on board." I and others tried to persuade him to stop on shore but he had made up his mind. I said "If we go back on board I am going to sea, I am not going to look at the shore." We were back on board and true to my word I hove up and set sail. Nobby was so angry that in his haste to beat me to it, he went out on the bowsprit and loosed the jib. There came a nice breeze from the NE and Nobby overhauled me on my weather quarter. I knew that if I made a tack he would be by me so held my stretch inside Cleeness and Haile Sand Fort. Nobby would not risk this and put about on to the starboard tack to get further to windward. I had just passed the fort when dense fog shut in. There was still a smart breeze and I knew that in my position I was clear of traffic. I put the log over and shaped my course. Seven hours later I picked up the Dudgeon Bell buoy and altered course. The wind and the fog held and there was a nasty kick in the sea. Timing my vessel and judging her speed with all hands continually peering we found the Cockle lightship after a further nine hours sail. The ebb tide was just coming to the north so that we were making slow progress. There were dozens of ships at anchor from the Cockle to Yarmouth Roads. We picked our way from anchor light to anchor light and anchored within a 100 yards of the harbour entrance. Next morning the tug came out for his usual look round, discovered us and towed us in. We were for Cantly. Nobby had anchored when the fog first came down but had a go later. He passed Yarmouth at 3 pm and was so confident that he was first that he hoisted his number to be reported. When he arrived at Margate and got on the phone the governor chided him with "When you pulled your colours up, Nobby, the *Hibernia* was unloaded."

Things came to a fine pass between us. We were at anchor off Greenhithe one Saturday, both bound to Yarmouth and had our usual arrangement. With a strong E wind, we knew that we could not do any good but decided to sail to the west shore river Medway, for a new hat. we set everything smart and started tacking down the river. Mr Everard sent a motorship down after us ordering us to return to Greenhithe and see him in the office. We did this and he said "I have had enough of this bally nonsense. They are my spars and my sails you'll blow away; shake hands and forget it." We did so and have been more or less amicable ever since.

76

In November 1930 I had my first spot of real bother. I had loaded sugar at Cantly and towed down to Yarmouth arriving there at about 2 pm. There was a little fog draught from the NW and I was told that four other barges had sailed that morning. I towed to sea to find a calm and dense fog outside. I drove to the southward with the flood tide for an hour and hearing numerous fog bells of ships at anchor ahead, ordered the anchor to be dropped. At 3 am the fog cleared with a full gale from the SSE. The normal charge for taking barges back in harbour once they had sailed was double towage rates: this on an average was £4 per barge at the time. At daybreak the tug was after the other four barges and they agreed to tow in for £10 for each barge. When he came to me we were dragging and I refused to tow in for fear the tug company would try and claim salvage. I could not get my anchor up to run her through the roads so let go my other anchor. I told the tug Skipper that if I wanted to go in harbour I would pull up flags for him. We finally brought up about a cable from the north pier and rode it out. At 4 pm I hoisted flags requesting a tug. He promptly came out and towed us in. The tug company sent in a bill for £10. which Mr Everard refused to pay thinking it excessive. The tug company took the case to court, won the day and got £100 not £10. Hereafter is my original deposition to the court which fully describes this particular incident.

JAMES ALFRED UGLOW WILL STATE:
On 18 June last I gave a statement to my Owners' lawyers and in that statement I set out the facts attaching to the services rendered to the *Hibernia* on 11 December last year. I did not in that statement set out my reasons why the occurrences mentioned therein occurred.
I might mention that I have a crew of three hands. During the early morning of 11 December, 1930, I myself was on watch. At about 3 am my barge commenced to drag; she was then in a position where I could not have sailed for the entrance to the Harbour owing to the barge *Gravelines* and a survey boat being anchored near me. I determined to let my barge drag clear of these craft and as I only then had twenty fathoms of cable on the port anchor I watched her while she dragged and then let out a few more fathoms and, as I thought, brought her up in such a position that she could sail for the entrance to Yarmouth at about slack water. I then went below and must

have fallen asleep by mistake for the next I knew was at about 5 am and I immediately went on deck and found that my barge had again commenced to drag and was out of position for sailing into Yarmouth. I paid out more cable but she still continued to drag and was in fact dragging slightly when the *Tactful* spoke me shortly before 6 am. I then came to the conclusion that it would be unwise to take any assistance from the *Tactful* for the weather was not too good and she had seen me dragging and was likely to claim salvage. I therefore refused assistance but while the *Tactful* was near by I dropped a second anchor and brought up. I did this really to show her that I was in a perfectly safe position but at the same time I admit that I had every intention of getting into Yarmouth during the course of the day for both my Mate and Third Hand are Yarmouth men and I much prefer being in shelter and ashore in bad weather. I therefore told the tug that if I required to enter the harbour later I would exhibit my signal which I in fact did at about 11 o'clock.

I might mention that when the tug spoke me at about 6 the tide was still running to the northward, being ebb and the sea was therefore a good deal smoother when the tide and wind were in the same direction that it was at 11 when the tide had turned and my barge also no doubt appeared to be more comfortable at 6 for at 11 she was going partially athwart and was of course rolling slightly and taking water on deck but there was literally no danger in this, particularly as she was absolutely steady and not dragging the slightest between 6 and 11 o'clock. I have no doubt in my own mind at all that I could have lain comfortably during the afternoon of 11 December and during the night the wind shot to the NW, which is off shore and I should therefore have been perfectly safe. If I had thought salvage services would have been claimed for I should most certainly have not entered the port.

I might mention that only about two months before this I lay through quite a bad gale at Corton Roads and although I did make a little water there was not the slightest danger to the ship or the cargo. I do not say that a sugar cargo would not have been slightly wetted in making water; it might have been but this certainly did not imperil ship and cargo.

I did not keep any logbook record of this accident and I did not report in writing to my owners but only over the telephone.

GEORGE E DRAY OF 94 MIDDLEGATE, YARMOUTH. STATES:
I was Mate on the *Hibernia* on 11 December last. I have heard the Master's Statement and quite agree with all he says so far as it concerns my views and the actual facts.

Previous to this I had had a heavy passage from Yarmouth to London but did it in the record time for a loaded barge of sixteen hours from Yarmouth to St Katherines Dock, London. We had finished loading sugar at Cantly at noon and I informed the owner that I was unable to get a tug to tow me down to Yarmouth that day. He replied "I want your ship in London, I will see there is a tug there for you." Sure enough at 2.30 pm the small tug *Gensteam* appeared and we proceeded to Yarmouth. It was blowing a full gale from the NNE with intermittent rain squalls and my intention had been to moor at Yarmouth for the night and see if the weather improved. To my surprise when we towed through Yarmouth bridge in the gathering gloom of the evening, the sea going tug *George Jewson* was waiting with navigation lights burning. The agent stood on the quay as we came alongside and said "Mr Will says you have got to proceed straight to sea." At this stage of my career wind and water never frightened me as it has sometimes done since, but I was incensed to think that I was not allowed to use my own judgement. I merely said "Before I proceed to sea I want those orders in writing." He agreed to return to the office and type them out for me. In the meantime I wrote a hurried letter of explanation to my sister in case of accidents and when I received the written orders, put them in the letter for him to post.
The *Hibernia* would not load herself down to her Plimsoll with sugar under hatches and we had a stack of bags three high on the hatches. This was covered with two tarpaulins which were well battened down to the combings. We towed out into the darkness and proceeded through Yarmouth Roads with only the foresail and skirt of the mainsail set, while I studied the situation. When we were clear of the Stanford channel off Lowestoft, she began to take a lot of water on board because she was not going fast enough to keep ahead of the sea. We

got the topsail and three quarters of the mainsail on her, set the standing jib and went tearing along in a smother of foam. Running up outside of the Gunfleet Sand we met the ebb tide which caused a short steep sea. The old *Hibernia* could not pick herself up quickly enough at times and a wall of water would hit the stack of sugar and go roaring forward and out through the space between the two hatchways where the mast was situated. She washed the side lights out and as it was not fit to risk a man's life to relight them, we proceeded without lights. We were in the Thames before daylight and went chasing up the river on the young flood tide. After docking I proceeded to the London Office and was told Mr Will wanted to see me in his room. Upon entering he asked me where I was at 2 am because he had woke up and thought about me. I explained the whys and wherefores and was told that in future I was to use my own discretion and take no risks.

For nearly a 100 years, the normal procedure for barges bound on a sea voyage had been to wait for an off shore or following wind and then proceed. It was seldom that a barge made a passage with the wind on the land unless it was fine settled weather. When I took charge of the *Hibernia*, Everard's fleet of coasters were beginning to open a new chapter in barging history by thrashing round the coast in fair wind or foul and making remarkable passages. This was partly due to sheer drive on the part of the owner and partly because he had good men capable of carrying out his wishes and orders. The fleet was well found in good gear and in return the Skippers were expected to use it to its fullest extent. Added to this was the natural rivalry between Skippers in a large firm, some friendly and some not so friendly. I personally have always got a thrill of satisfaction when beating the other man or men on passage. This is a thrill that nobody in a power driven ship can possibly have. Under canvas it is personal achievement which puts one vessel ahead of another, a knowledge of one's ship and how to load her and trim her sails to varying conditions to obtain the greatest speed. With power it is only a question of the size of the propeller and how many revolutions can be obtained from the engine.

I have said in a previous chapter that barge racing is a different and distinct thing from barge sailing. When racing one not only does one's best to get every inch out of one's own barge but also does all one can to blanket or stop the other competitors. There are very few barges alike in their sailing vagaries. On the *Glenmore,* Captain Brooks had found by years of experience that she would go to windward fastest with the mainsheet pinned in like a bar and the vang or peak hand taut. I found that the *Hibernia* used to like a foot of sheet eased off. While racing the *Cambria,* Nobby Finch proved that she liked her sail with a good flow in it and used to ease as much as three feet of sheet off so that the sail looked right out of her. It used to make her go however.

Balance on the rudder, so that a barge does not drag a lot of lee helm apart from trimming the sails, depends mainly on the judicious placing of the leeboard. I have found in the few barges that I have sailed that the foresail is a burying sail and the jib a lifting one. Especially in strong winds. The *Hibernia* in particular would drop her old lee jaw down and go gnawing into the wind with the foresail set in a breeze. Drop the foresail down and up would come her head with a consequent easing of the weight on the rudder.

Although it has been the fashion to place large mule rigged mizens in coasting barges, they are a pressing sail to windward and what you gain by carrying the mizen in a breeze is more than lost by the weight of water against the rudder. I later proved this particular point in the *Will Everard.* I had been in company with Jimmy Mole of the *Alf Everard.* We had a fair sail from the Humber to Harwich with each of us sailing our hardest and very little to choose between the two vessels. We both had a coal cargo from Keadby to Margate but had orders to go into Harwich until we were required at Margate. We were given permission to continue some three days later. We mustered from Harwich at about four hours ebb with a strong wind W by S. Jimmy was out clear first and we went chasing off to the Long Sand Head buoy, with the wind on the starboard quarter and all sail crammed on. We were about three lengths behind him when we pinned our sheets and hauled up round the buoy. The first thing after that was to haul our big flying jib down and stow it before it pulled the topmast out of her. Jimmy doing the same practically simultaneously. We held up close to the wind between the Long Sand to windward and the Kentish Knock to leeward. By doing this we could just about fetch the NE spit buoy distant twenty five miles. They were both making hard work of it for the man at the wheel. We were still our three lengths astern at the end of five miles but I had been observing the *Alf Everard's* rudder. It was first pressed practically hard to port then eased a little and then back but always to port. I said "Furl our mizen and see what happens." As soon as the mizen was off her we carried our rudder amidships and crept ahead. I bore away well clear of the *Alf* so that he would not steal my wind and passed through his lee. Jimmy still kept his mizen set but by the time we approached Margate, the *Will* was half a mile ahead and without any hard work at the wheel.

Reverting to the *Hibernia* another exploit of which I was very proud at the time was of getting her out of Southwold Harbour with a nice breeze straight in the pier heads. I had never previously been in Southwold and had orders to load coal for there from Keadby. We were abreast of the town at about four hours flood and just right for the tide. There was a smart breeze from the SW which meant that we could enter with a free sheet. As I was unacquainted with the place I hoisted a flag for a pilot. When abreast of the harbour the pilot boarded us from a small motor fishing boat and we proceeded into harbour without incident.

We had not got an agent in the port which meant I was responsible for paying the pilot and harbour dues. The pilot was evidently one of the careful kind because as soon as we were moored he presented his bill to me. I scrutinised it and saw "To use of motor boat 30/-." I pointed out that we had sailed in without the aid of a motorboat and he said it was the usual procedure. If there was a breeze when we wanted to leave the port they would put two motorboats on to tow us for the same charge. This seemed reasonable and I paid. When we were unloaded, I had orders to proceed straight back to Keadby. There was a nice breeze ESE and I knew that if I could get clear of the harbour I would have a fair wind. I approached the pilot and requested the use of the two motorboats as promised. He said he was sorry but there was too much jump at the piers and the motorboats being of shallow draft, their propellers would not grip the water sufficiently to pull us out. He also informed me that I would have to wait for a change of wind to leave the harbour with. This aroused my fighting insticts and after a swear off I told him I would leave that tide without any assistance.

I walked out on to the north pier head and observed a big

wooden sheave set up on the end of the pier. Evidently in years gone by vessels had warped out of the harbour. There were several camps about — it was mid-summer — and while we had been discharging there had been an admiring audience of boy scouts. I approached the scout master and the leader of some youth club and explained that I wanted as many tons of humanity as I could get to warp us out of the harbour. They were only too keen to oblige. We bent all the 2½ inch rope we could find on board together and got a length of 180 fathoms. One end was made fast to the port bow cleat and the other end tailed round the sheave on the pier head. I waited until the first of the tide started running out of the harbour, set the sails smart and gave my volunteers the order to pull. There were about a hundred of them tailed on, including some fishermen. As we approached the outer end of the piers the shore end of the line was thrown aboard aft and the Third Hand hauled in the slack as we went ahead. They gave us good way and at the right moment I shouted "Let go" and we filled off on the starboard tack. There was one sickening moment as she jumped her chine down about three feet clear of the concrete base of the pier and then we were out clear. I passed Nobby in the *Cambria* bound south in the Stanford Channel. We hailed each other and he shouted "Where are you from?" I laconically answered "Southwold," and he flung back "You .... liar. You couldn't have got out of there." This pleased me greatly, I could forgive him for doubting my veracity.

In those days I did not always let my choice of wind and weather take me to sea. Sometimes the state of my pocket was the main consideration. I was earning good money and spending it. One case in point was when we were stone loaded from Plymouth to London. I had subbed well on the passage down channel having put into Poole to get a buckled crosstree straightened. I drew more money at Plymouth and with the assistance of the Mate, soon got rid of it. I daren't ask for more. Mr Everard knew when his Skippers were on the binge by the amount of money they drew.

There was a fresh east wind and having only 2/- left I decided to proceed. It took us 60 hours of thrashing to get to the Isle of Wight. In the broken water off St Albans, she threw me right over the top of the wheel and my left leg went green and blue from thigh to knee. I had to anchor off Ryde for two days to get over it. Even then we had to turn the rest of the passage.

By 1930, the Dutch motor coasters were a real menace on the British coast. They had the run of our coasts and had cut freights to practically rock bottom. Freights were scarce and competition keen and even if a merchant had a sense of patriotism he was not likely to pay a high rate of freight to a sailing barge that could not guarantee a delivery date, when he could get a fast motorship to do it cheaper. To illustrate this, I was in John Carter's office, the Shipbrokers at Poole, Dorset, one morning. We were discharging a cargo of cement and I had been given orders to proceed to Bridport to load grit for Deptford Creek, London. The rate of freight was 8/6d per ton, crew to trim cargo. At the time this was quite a good figure and I was pleased to get the cargo. There was the skipper-owner of a Dutch coaster in the office and a freight on offer from Bridport to Barton Haven opposite Hull. Both ports are bad for water and the price should have been a good one. The agents said "I have a telegram here it reads 'Rate of freight 6/- per ton, may pay 7/-." The Dutchman immediately replied "Fix it, fix it." The agent said "We can hold out for the other shilling." Again came the reply "Fix it." The Dutchman turned to me and asked for some information concerning Bridport. I was so disgusted that I uncharitably replied "B. . . . . well find out from somebody else."

The Dutch government were subsidising the building of these coasters and the banks would advance 80 per cent of the purchase price to a good many, the same as one would have a house built in Britain. Most of these craft were family concerns and besides being their ship it was also their home. The skipper's wife was usually a member of the crew. As long as they could pay the interest off their loan they seemed quite content. They were not popular with bargemen.

We sailed for Bridport and loaded our cargo. While loading it blew hard from the southward which formed a bar of shingle across the entrance. We had to lay a week before the ebb tide from the harbour was strong enough to wash this bar away. This is no unusual occurence at Bridport.

At this time it was already becoming increasingly difficult to get crews. The main two reasons being that life was easier on-board motorships—there was no hauling and heaving—and also the curse of the Dole. Experienced Mates were leaving to go into power craft and you could not get youngsters to train on because they could get 15/- per week on the dole. We could only afford to pay 15/- per week and food as wages and the majority preferred to let Dad keep them and have their dole for pocket money.

George Dray was an excellent Mate and could get a good meal ready in record time as well as attending to his other duties. 1931 was our best year and for the greater part of it we were only two handed. The *Hibernia* was a big barge to work two handed but we managed. I do not think our record that year has ever been equalled. We did thirty complete cargoes on the coast, the shortest voyage being to Lowestoft from London. Most of the others were either to the Humber or down channel—Southampton, Newport, Poole, Bridport, Plymouth and Par. We were both young and vigorous and our luck held. When we were ready for sea, if the wind was dead against us, we used to proceed with the knowledge that it could not come any worse. Once out clear of the land we used to pick the tack that would let us lay nearest to our proper course and hold on to it as long as possible. The wind would either free out so that we could haul up to it or back, in which case we were to windward.

In February we loaded 100 tons of linseed from London to Southampton. There was little doing in London and I knew that if I returned there empty we would probably lay for a week. There was on offer at Southampton a cargo of loam from Hamble to Plymouth and I obtained Mr Everard's permission to fix it. The weather had been dirty with the wind from the SW but just before we were ready it veered NW. As soon as we were loaded we set sail. We fetched about eight miles wide of Portland Bill and well outside the race. The wind backed steadily and we made Berry Head on the other tack. By the time we had worked down to Start Point, the wind was WSW strong, thick with rain and a huge sea. The seas were so high and long that when she dropped into the trough we could not feel the wind. We had sailed at 9 am of one day and at 5 am the next morning I stood into the land as close as I dared. Visibility was poor and the hand lead was practically useless because the cliffs on this part of the coast are steep to. I then stood off on the starboard tack. Being wet through I decided to go below for a dry change leaving George at the wheel. While changing I could hear the fog horn of a big ship approaching. I scrambled my clothes on as fast as I could and went on deck. George trying to steer and blow our hand fog horn single handed, had let us come up head to wind. We commenced paying head inshore just as the lights of a large ship loomed up ahead and to starboard. The only thing to do to avoid a collision was to let the vang and main sheet fly and try to wear her round. This was done shipping a hell of a sea in the middle of the manoeuvre. George scrambled along the deck and hove up on the main brails. My dry clothes had availed me but little, the unlucky sea we caught saturating the pair of us. We were now headed back up channel and the danger was past. I swore aloud and asked what a ship that size was doing so close to the land. I then said something I should not have done: it was, "I hope he goes ashore putting the wind up me like that." I watched the ship's lights disappear judging his course and then said "The way he is going he stands a damned good chance of piling her up." It proved to be one of the 'Ben' boats the *Benmoor* and half an hour afterwards the Skipper piled her up on Prawle Point.

I decided to run back to allow us to get some dry clothes on and a meal. It was coming daybreak and George asked where we were going being unacquainted with this part of the coast. I said "I'll show you a pretty little harbour called Darmouth." Show him was all I did for by the time we reached the entrance both wind and tide were out. In under the cliffs the wind was puffy and fluky. The rain had cleared and the weather seemed to be moderating. I made several tacks between the Mewstone and Blackstone Rocks. George was not enamoured with this performance and suggested we have another go at getting to Plymouth. I agreed and as she came round on to the port tack kept the foresail to the mast on the bowline and hove-to. We took it in turns to get some sleep and after another night out arrived at Plymouth. When I walked into the agent's office he asked me if I had towed down channel. On being told "No" he congratulated me saying they had been expecting three schooners for weeks and we had only been 70 hours.

We discharged 70 tons in Millbay Dock and proceeded to Devonport Dockyard with the other 100 tons. The next morning we uncovered the hatches ready for discharging. Somebody came round and said "Are you all ready Skipper?" I said "Yes, when you are. Where are the gangs?" "We only provide the crane and shovels" was the reply, also "The crew

Skipper of Hibernia

has to unload." There was nothing for it but for the Skipper and 'crew' to start shovelling, both of us. The cargo was foundry loam, and it says much for our adaptability for we shovelled the whole 100 tons into large buckets in two and a half days. At the end of that period there were two aching men that temporarily had lost interest in going on shore.

We next proceeded to Forder Creek, an inlet from the River Tamar, to load road stone for London. We sailed to the entrance of the creek, where I had made arrangements for a motor boat to meet us. To get to the loading berth we had to pass through the arch of a tall narrow bridge. The arch was about sixty feet high and this necessitated lowering the topmast. An hour before high water there was no sign of any motor boat to tow us in—it afterwards transpired that it had broken down—so I decided to sail in. The wind was blowing straight into the creek so we only set the foresail and in she went. We were empty and it was practically high water. As we approached the arch I shouted to the Mate who was standing forward "Is she going to clear?" I was thinking of our sprit end. First he answered "Yes" and as we got a little closer, "She won't do it." She did, must to the amazement of the quarrymen who were watching us. I would not have liked to have been sitting on the end of the sprit.

We loaded a varied and smelly lot of cargoes that year. Our next order was to proceed to the entrance of Barking Creek and load a cargo of guano for the 'Dutch River' at Goole. The guano was in the hold of a full rigged sailing ship that had brought it from the islands off Peru. It was a filthy, evil smelling cargo and I was not pleased to find that we were expected to trim our own cargo. We did, however, and the reek of ammonia was so strong that although we tied handkerchiefs round our nostrils and mouths, we could only stay in the hold for a quarter of an hour at a time. We loaded two of these cargoes during the year and made record passages on both. The wooden bulkheads separating the focsle and cabin from the hold were neither air nor smell proof. I noticed a curious thing in this connection. With the wind aft the smell would come back against the wind into the cabin and when we were head to wind it would go forward and the cabin would smell comparatively sweet. It rained while we were discharging and a lot of muck was left on the beams and lining of the hold.

We then sailed from Goole to Keadby to load coal for Cantly Sugar Works. We normally towed up the River Trent but at this time pylons for the electric grid system were being erected across the river. To make certain that these pylons and the connecting wires were placed high enough to ensure unrestricted navigation, Mr Will Everard insisted that his barges sail up the river.

After the coal we had a cargo of sugar for London. This meant the hold had to be scrubbed out. A laborious business. Every bucket of water had to be drawn from over the side by hand and when the hold was clean, all this water had to be pumped from the bilges also by hand. In April, we loaded rice from London to Yarmouth. We arrived off Yarmouth at midnight with a strong east wind and too much sea to enter the harbour without the assistance of a tug. I sailed off under the lee edge of the Scroby Sand and anchored. I went well inside the Scroby Elbow buoy where I knew we could lay in smooth water. At 11 am the wind having moderated, I decided to set the sails and proceed back to the harbour. As soon as we set the sails the Master of the St Nicholas Lightship, with more enthusiasm than sense, had a maroon fired to indicate to the shore that we were in distress. I suppose from the angle between the two vessels he could see broken water with us apparently in the middle of it. We were proceeding up through the roads in comfort when I was amazed to see four lifeboats and a tug approaching us. The Lowestoft boat, the Gorleston and also Caister and Palling lifeboats. It would have been laughable if one of the Lowestoft men had not dropped dead while running to take his place in the lifeboat. It did, however, bring the tug out of the harbour more promptly than usual and after assuring himself that there were no pickings to be had that day, the Master of the tug took our tow rope.

In the month of May we created a record doing four clear cargoes and two round trips to the Humber in the month: cement from Wouldham, River Thames to Lowestoft then empty from Lowestoft to Keadby; from there, coal for Margate back to Wouldham to load cement, part cargo for Lowestoft and part cargo for Norwich; then once more empty to Keadby and more coal for Margate. One week we put in 127 hours sailing time without the work attached to loading and discharging. Our luck still held and we proceeded to Queenborough to load artificial fertilizer for Newport, IOW.

Skipper of Hibernia

We arrived at Cowes an hour before high water one day and
the tides were neaping. We had no time to get the bowsprit
topped up out of the way but went tearing up the River
Medina with everything set. I knew she wouldn't go too far. As
luck would have it, she sailed right into her berth and stopped
dead. There was no need to worry about check ropes for she
had come up out of the water a foot.

All that year we were chasing about like a handsaw. I do not
remember laying one day for weather. I was to be married on
Boxing Day and was getting some cash together to furnish our
home which probably explains a lot. I had kept to my original
resolution to be a lone wolf as far as possible and found it paid
dividends. While discharging rice at Yarmouth I had twenty-
three teeth extracted at one sitting, came out of the dentists at
3 pm and went to the pictures. I finished up by getting in-
toxicated on brandy and milk but went to sea at 6 next morning.

We went on the ways three days before Christmas to be fitted
with a new suit of sails ready for the Thames Barge Race the
following year. I lowered the gear down and unbent the old
sails and then given permission to take a week off to get
married and have a short honeymoon. I married a girl from
Hull who has proved a faithful and house-proud partner. In
this narrative I have made little mention of my experiences on
land; I will content myself by saying that I have a good wife,
two fine sons and a nice home and I am proud of all of them.

While I was on leave the *Hibernia* was fitted with a new
foresail, topsail and mainsail. We had always used wire head
ropes in the mainsails in Everards, but this sail had the old
fashioned rope headrope. The elder school of bargemen con-
tended that there was more give in a rope headrope and that
when the sail was dry the headrope and canvas would stretch
together and conversely when wet would shrink together. In
this case it proved very unsatisfactory at sea. Through sailing
on the coast in heavy weather, and also through heaving the
vangs in tight when at anchor to prevent the sprit jerking, the
headrope stretched so much that it burst away from the canvas. The owners advised that when at anchor in a seaway, the
weight should be kept from the head rope by heaving up on
the yard tackle: that is, a tackle leading from the middle of
the sprit to the mast head and from there to the deck. I tried
this several times and found that it merely produced a huge

bow in the sprit and that the latter could not be held steady. I have lain athwart the sea in an open roadstead, when the barge has rolled so heavily that beside heaving the vang falls in taut on the winches. I have had to put a tackle athwartships on the two vangs and then fasten a 3 cwt anchor on to the running part of the tackle to prevent the sprit jerking. I contend that there is sufficient stretch and spring in flexible steel wire for the purpose of a headrope to a mainsail. The only thing is that the canvas must be properly stretched before being sewn on the headrope.

On the other hand I am a firm believer in wooden spars. These have the necessary give in them. We had tried a steel sprit in the *Hibernia* but in a seaway it was dead and when tacking would swing to leeward with a jerk with a consequent detrimental effect on the mainsail. When gybing a wooden sprit will bend after taking the initial weight and there is an easing on the strain on the vang. With the steel sprit I found that I had to renew the $2\frac{3}{4}$ inch rope vang falls every three months instead of the normal twelve months. Later when I took charge of the *Will Everard* I introduced the idea of flexible steel wire for the main shroud lanyards. The *Will* is so heavy on her gear that with the usual four strand 3 inch tarred hemp lanyards she would continually stretch them. This meant setting the rigging up nearly every trip and by the time the lanyards had finished stretching they had had their day. The older school were dubious about this innovation saying it would lift the top of the barge. There may be some justification for this point of view in the case of wooden barges grounding in a bad berth because a wooden barge will bend all shapes if she sits awkwardly. I once saw the *Glenmore* push her plank ends half an inch aft of her transom on the starboard side due to a bad berth. When she refloated she went back into shape. To refer back to mainsails with a rope headrope, when the sail is first bent or rigged, the peak of the sail is not put over the sprit end but lashed to the sprit about eighteen inches from the top of the sprit, the idea being that with the peak in this position the sail will stretch gradually and setting in on the sheet will give an even pull on both leach and footrope. If the sail was placed directly over the sprit end the downward pull would be so as to stretch the leach out of proportion to the rest of the sail. With a wire headrope the best practice is to place the sail over the sprit end and then slack the collar lashing at the throat of the sail and merely have the mast rope seasoned to the jackstay temporarily instead of using shackles. When the sail has stretched, usually a period of three months, it is rigged into its permanent position.

The usual cause of a slack leach on a topsail is through crews pulling the topsail sheet out to its fullest extent and then taking up on the head of the sail. The correct way to set a topsail is to leave the sheet slack until the head of the sail is in the required position then take the tack taut and last of all set the sheet home. This fault in setting a topsail is the main reason why most barges carry their topmast stayed forward of the perpendicular. The leach stretches out of proportion to the rest of the sail and to prevent it flapping the topmast is stayed forward. This practice of staying the topmast forward is a disadvantage when carrying a flying jib or jib topsail, and has been the cause of many broken topmasts. Another cause of broken topmasts is having the standing backstays too tight. If the main rigging is a little slack, an advantage I think, the head of the mainsail in a breeze will be inches to leeward of the centre of the barge. If the standing backstays are not slacked in proportion the head of the topmast is held to windward causing the spar to bow to leeward. It only wants that extra puff of wind and the middle of the spar will fly out.

I overstayed my leave by three days and then put in an appearance at Greenhithe. The *Hibernia* was fully rigged, afloat and loaded with a cargo of rice meal for Hull. I reported to Mr Will Everard who greeted me with "Are you alright Uglow?" When I replied in the affirmative he said "Well bally well get off afloat and tell that other man to come ashore before he takes your ship away." I went on board and sure enough there was another Skipper on board who had orders to take her to Hull. I was buying my house on the never-never principle and after having paid for furniture and installed my wife in our future home this had left us with 50/- as our total capital. This meant that the *Hibernia* had not got to lose any time in getting to Hull. She didn't, and we had a rousing passage with a gale of wind from the SW, much to the detriment of my new mainsail. Due to the great strain the roping and canvas stretched far too quickly and by the time we were at Cromer, the sail had come down so far that it was sweeping the deck. We had to heave upon the main brails to take the leach in and lift the foot of the sail.

SAILORMAN

I had a sickening experience on this passage. I was standing at the wheel when the dawn came and the barge was abeam of Cromer. I was dressed in wool pants and vest, woollen stockings and leather kneeboots, trousers and two thick woollen jerseys topped by a jacket fastened with two safety pins in lieu of buttons. As the light grew stronger, I saw a big black rat scuttle along the deck. It had evidently come on board when the cargo was loaded. I shouted to George the Mate to close the focsle and cabin companion ways and try and catch the rat. He chased it along the deck and it ran into the open fronted wheelhouse. Before I realised what was happening it ran up the back of my legs and inside the back of my jacket. I let go of the wheel shouting like a madman and dashed out on to the port quarter. I could feel the rat struggling to get out and I was struggling equally furiously to get the safety pins undone and my jacket off. I had just succeeded in getting them adrift when the rat squirmed up through the collar and jumped to the deck. George killed it with a piece of wood and I jumped it to pulp swearing like a trooper because of the fright it had given to me.

Our cargo was consigned to Calemill at Stoneferry, well up what is known as Old Harbour. This is really the River Hull and it is not generally known that the correct name for Hull is Kingston-upon-Hull. The tides ran strongly in the River Hull and as there are several bridges to pass through and not sufficient width to swing a vessel, craft proceed up the river stern first. The usual procedure and the one we adopted on this particular voyage, is to employ a tug which tows you stern first with a tow rope leading from each quarter of the vessel being towed. Vessels have their main anchor on the ground with sufficient cable to keep them head upon tide but a short enough scope of cable to allow the tug to drag the anchor over the bottom. The ships boat is also kept handy forward for one of the crew to scull a line ashore if necessary to check the vessel at the various bridges.

We completed our passage and getting a fine day while the cargo was being discharged we set the rigging up. The new shroud lanyards had stretched badly. We also shortened the standlift up a couple of links. This is a wire stay with several large steel links in its lower end which leads from the hounds at the top of the mast to the lower end of the sprit. It is shackled to the fore eye on a three eyed band at the base of the sprit. The other two eyes are shackled to a semi-circular steel plate round the aft side of the main mast. This is known as the muzzle and it holds the lower end of the sprit to the mast. By taking up on the standlift we lifted the sprit bodily which took the peak of the mainsail up to the requisite height to allow the sail to set smartly.

We were fortunate enough to load a return cargo of a different grade of meal, from the same factory which we were discharging. This return cargo was consigned to Bow Creek, London. I had a double incentive to get a move on with this cargo. I was returning home to my newly wed wife and I had the money in my pocket to pay off some of the mortgage on my house. Once clear of Hull, we proceded down the River Humber with a strong SW wind. By the time we had crossed Lynn Well and got under the lee of the Norfolk coast at Blakeny the wind had backed to S by E and was blowing a full gale. We were reduced to storm jib, foresail and mainsail and could barely lay our course. It was pitch dark and we were making heavy weather of it so I decided to anchor abreast of Sheringham and close inshore.

We did this and pulled at the end of a taut cable for twelve hours. The wind then veered to about W by S and moderated a little. We scrambled under way and made fast time to Corton Roads to the north of Lowestoft. The wind still held W by S so I decided to hold my stretch and try and fetch Orfordness. I observed the anchor lights of a small motor ship anchored in Corton Roads and later found that it was one of our firms ships the M V *Prowess.* In the previous nights gale bound up channel for London, the wind and sea had proved so strong that the Master of the *Prowess* could not hold her to the land rounding the North Foreland and had to let her blow to leeward until he anchored in Corton Roads. I was unaware of this at the time and also that the rest of the barge fleet including the four big Everard's were weather bound in Yarmouth, laden with sugar for London. Some of them had been in there for three weeks. We had plenty of water come on board but fetched Orfordness and kept close hauled on the starboard tack until we came to the Sunk Head buoy.

The weather was very unsettled and dirty and the wind now commenced to back steadily towards south again and increasing all the time. I didn't mind so much as I had got a little shelter from the Sunk Sand and every mile I worked to the SW the various sand banks in the Thames Estuary gave me greater protection. By the time we got to the Maplin Spit it was night again and we were under reduced canvas. The wind from the SSW blowing a gale and a strong flood tide made a short steep sea that *Hibernia* did not like one little bit. She took every other one straight across her and both the ship and her crew were in their usual state of saturation. The wind backed still further until it was due south and we were able to fetch away on the port tack. In another two hours we were at the Nore and smoking up Sea Reach. We berthed early the following morning and I learned that we would be three days discharging.

I informed the Owners of the position and went home. I returned on board before the cargo was completely discharged and was ordered to proceed empty to Greenhithe and that I was to be ashore to see Mr Will at 8 am the next morning. I was to learn next morning that the *Will Everard* was at anchor off Greenhithe and that her Skipper had blotted his copy book and failed to give satisfaction to the Owners. I went ashore at 8 and heard Mr Will inform the Skipper of the *Will* of all his shortcomings and tell him that he would have to take a smaller ship. He then turned to me and in no pleasant tone said, "As for you, get on board that *Will Everard* and take her up to the Millwall Dock to load cake for Lynn." I said in surprise "Do you mean go Skipper of the *Will*?" and he replied "Yes, get your gear on board and don't be long about it." So on 6 February 1932 I was Skipper of one of the four largest sailing barges ever built. It was two months after my twenty-sixth birthday and I had reached the summit of my ambition. My only regret was that I had reached it by the relegation of another man. I would have much preferred that the former Skipper had been promoted to one of the power ships.

CHAPTER **6**

Will Everard

Before I proceed with my story of the *Will Everard,* I would like to say that I have always endeavoured to keep a clean ship, if not a smart one. In our firm it is not easy to keep a ship smart and newly painted. The only time the ships go on to the ways for a good overhaul is once in four years when they are due for this examination under Lloyds. The annual survey is usually a very cursory affair and as long as all the ship's equipment and hatches are sound, the ship is surveyed and away the same day. The firm have only limited facilities for repairs and such a large fleet that it is one constant rush to chase one ship off to make room for the next. Apart from loading and discharging, when little can be done, the Mate is usually tallying the cargo if bag stuff and all the fine weather time is spent under way. If you have to put into harbour with contrary winds it is usually raining, although when weather bound is usually the only opportunity for painting. Apart from this a ship can be kept decently clean. I have never tried to treat my crew as I was treated as a youngster and as long as they keep the ship decent, let them go their own way. I have one fad however and that is a hatred of 'Irish pennants' and 'rats' tails'—loose pieces of spunyarn hanging from the rigging and ropes without whipped ends. It is curious how the best of present day Mates will walk along the deck a hundred times and never think of tucking in a frayed end of spunyarn that has chafed adrift from the serving covering a splice of a wire. I like to see serving kept tarred, ratlines parallel to each other and running ropes kept taut and coiled. Nothing looks worse to a real bargeman than mooring ropes heaped all over the hatchway on deck. On the

95

other hand nothing looks smarter than each rope neatly coiled, Flemish coiled for preference if there is room. A good Mate is essential for the smooth working of the ship. He will not only carry out his own numerous duties but also keep the other hand or hands busy.

The four big *Everards* were the only barges I knew to make a practice of sailing four handed. They were large craft and three men and a boy were not too many when it came to manning the windlass. The *Will Everard* was one of the first of four sister ships all completed in a period of two years. They were built by Fellowes Limited of Great Yarmouth to Mr Everard's design and specification. Four stouter built barges never put to sea. The *Will* was 97 feet 6 inches from stem to sternpost in length, 23 feet 1 inch beam and 9 feet 9 inches moulded depth amidships; she had a hoist of 100 feet from topmast truck to deck and her huge sprit was 64 feet from end to end and 16 inches through the middle. She carried 5000 square feet of canvas in her foresail, topsail, mainsail and mizen. This does not include jibs, spinnaker or balloon foresail. Until converted her gross register tonnage was 189.3 and her net tonnage 150.85.

A curious anomaly was that although the four barges were built to the same specification, the *Will* and the *Ethel* were over the 150 tons net register and the *Alf* and *Fred* under 150 tons. They all carried an equal amount of cargo and in various harbours, notably Great Yarmouth, the *Will* and the *Fred* had to pay twice the amount of dues as the other two—and dearer towage rates as well.

When I first took charge of the *Will*, Jimmy Mole was Master of the *Alf Everard*, Jesse Farthing ('Four a Penny') was Master of the *Fred* and Tommy Willis Master of the *Ethel*. Jimmy Mole, now Master of the MV *Signality*, I considered the finest bargeman of my generation. He is eight years my senior and we are good friends. From 1932 to 1938 we had some hard sails against each other but it was all done in a good spirit and Jimmy was always ready to lend a helping hand. He made some remarkable passages in the *Alf*, notably forty-eight hours from Weymouth to Hull and twenty-eight hours from Hull to Margate. On another occasion he had discharged a cargo at Par in Cornwall. The *Alf* finished discharging at 2 pm on a Friday. When Jimmy phoned for orders, Mr Will said "I want you in London for Monday's work. Can you manage it?" Jimmy cockily replied "What is the matter with being home for Sunday dinner?" He sailed her up channel in a westerly gale and had his Sunday dinner at home. He is short, dark and stockily built and can turn his hand to practically anything. His present hobby is repairing clocks and watches and he is quite good at it. I have known him make his sons clothes when they were young and do all the family washing.

We were together at Keadby on one occasion awaiting our turn to load. I had had a stiff passage and there was a large rent in my mainsail from the headrope half way down the sail. Jimmy brought his Mate over unasked and said "Come on, let's get that gear down and I will spong that sail up for you." We lowered the spars practically to the deck and Jimmy started sewing. I am not much good with a needle and Jimmy did five feet to my one. He made as good a job of it as any sailmaker and then helped us rig again. When I thanked him his only comment was "That's worth a pint, let's go ashore." We did and had several pints.

Jesse was another of the 'Four Musketeers', always ready to go to sea and take a chance, or equally willing to stay in harbour and have a pint. We have all had exciting passages and good fun together.

Tommy Willis was the other one of the four, a chap of my own age who although he is now Master of the MV *Apricity* has still got his heart in the barges. For some unknown reason the *Ethel* was the cinderella of the four barges. Long after the other three had new suits of sails the *Ethel* carried on with her original suit. They were constantly being repaired and Tommy as Master had the work of lowering down the masts to have the repairs effected. Tommy's average number of freights in a year was not up to the average of the other three but only for the reason that he knew every time he had to sail in a real breeze, it meant lowering down and more work. His heart was practically broken when in 1940, after a really good overhaul, he was ordered to proceed to Dover to load stores for Dunkirk at the time of the evacuation. Tommy obeyed instructions and grounded his ship near Malo les Bains and after being dive bombed for several hours, was ordered to abandon his ship. The Navy put a demolition charge into her and left her. There has never been any trace of her found although I have seen photographs of her intact after the Germans had captured Dunkirk. Tommy still thinks that she was thrown away and also that he could have got her off given the opportunity.

Many a sailing craft has been lost through poor ground tackle, that is anchors and cables. With on shore gales in open roadsteads many a good ship has dragged ashore and broken up. I found when I took charge of the *Will* that the owners had erred on the other side. Her main port bower, the anchor usually used by bargemen was $9\frac{1}{2}$ cwt. This was shackled to sixty fathoms of one inch short link tested cable. Her second bower weighed 7 cwts and also had sixty fathoms of one inch cable. During my career in the *Will* I lost four of these heavy anchors simply because they held too well. If you let go the anchor and the bottom was blue clay you knew that there was going to be a devil of a job to break it out of the ground when it was time to heave up. Tacking to windward with a smart breeze against a three to four knot tide a barge will not make headway. The usual practice, in rivers or at sea if there is not too much swell, is to anchor under these circumstances, when the tide comes against you. Thus saving five or six hours unnecessary steering, it also gives the crew a chance to get some sleep on a long passage.

The *Will* had originally been fitted with a patent windlass. This had not proved a success. When I took her, this windlass had just been replaced by the old fashioned single gear Gardiner windlass. With the patent windlass with two gears the windlass handles would take nearly half a turn before they caught. A former Mate of the *Will* had a bad accident when heaving up anchor in a seaway. As the vessels head surged up out of the water and the weight came on the cable with a jerk, the windlass handle flew back and crowned him. Another time while running before the wind to the nor'ard of Orfordness, the foresail was flapping to and fro under the lee of the mainsail. The foot of the foresail kept knocking the brake on the windlass until it released it. The anchor not being bowed went down with a run. The barge was going through the water at a good speed and before anything could be done the full length of the cable tore over the windlass and disappeared.

With these huge anchors, the heaviest work on the *Will* was heaving up the anchor. The same thing applied to all four of the big 'uns and at different times we have all had a good swear off when after heaving our guts out and getting the anchor nearly to the surface, the anchor has run away. This used to occur when the wooden welts on the windlass were getting worn or when the windlass was greasy with mud. The first anchor I lost on the edge of the Sizewell Bank, off Aldborough. The wind was SW and we were bound to Margate. The barge began to loose ground as the ebb tide came away. As it was fairly smooth I decided to anchor. This we did in six fathoms of water. The wind freshened causing a short jumpy sea. When it was time to get under way we hove the cable short and set the sails. We were four handed and two of us were heaving on each windlass handle. We could not break the anchor out of the ground and the cable kept slipping round the barrel of the windlass. I took an extra turn round the barrel with the bight of the cable to prevent this slipping. Instead of the anchor breaking out the cable parted. After this experience I used to bow my anchor when leaving harbour and seldom attempted to let go before I had reached my destination. We used to tack about the English channel and the North Sea both ebb and flood even if it meant losing a couple of miles at the end of six hours hard sailing. We then had a 7 cwt anchor which held well and which we could get up in all normal weather. The secret of a good anchor is not so much the weight as the shape. I believe in an anchor with sharp heart shaped flukes not too broad and a long shank.

I was inclined to be nervous when we set sail to proceed up river for my first cargo in the *Will*. There was a fresh westerly wind straight down the river and the *Will* looked very cumbersome to me after my smart *Hibernia*. I had only made four tacks across the river however, when my confidence returned for she handled like a top. I was later to find that loaded ship, with her large and weighty cargo, she would shoot a lot further than the *Hibernia* when tacking—that is she would not come round so quickly but would carry her way all the time.

After loading in the Millwall Dock, we made a normal voyage in average time being just under the month on the two cargoes. From Margate my orders were to proceed to Brightlingsea to load beach shingle for Grimsby. This was my first experience of beach work. The barges used to moor on the beach athwart the foreshore with the main anchor leading into deep water forward and a kedge anchor aft. There were not any mooring posts and to hold the craft in the correct position until they grounded an unusual practice was

SAILORMAN

adopted. We had to dig two holes in the beach, one abreast of the bow and one abreast of the quarter, then bury a barrow and make our mooring lines fast to the wheel of the barrow. We carried out this performance and the attendant labour involved only to find that the mobile crane used for loading had not enough hoist to get into the hold of the *Will*. As we were unable to load I had to proceed empty to Keadby for another Margate cargo. This job done we proceeded to London and were occupied for three weeks giving her a good and necessary overhaul on the way.

Our old sailmaker at this time was a dabster at repairing sails but very loth to make new ones. If you blew a sail away and went ashore with the remnants under one arm old Jack would repair it. When I first went Skipper of the *Hibernia* she had an oft repaired topsail that was always tearing as soon as we were caught in a breeze of wind. After having to unbend this sail for repairs about six times in as many months, I determined he would not repair it again. The next time it tore I let it blow to pieces and when we arrived at Greenhithe took the bare roping ashore. Jack promptly proceded to make a new topsail using the old rope. When I complained to Mr Fred Everard he only said "We will make you a new one, that other one will come in for a spare." Having a large fleet of barges at this time we were never held up for sails as there were plenty of spares. I have blown a topsail away at the Dudgeon and ran back to the shelter of Yarmouth Roads, then gone ashore to report by telephone to be told "We are sending a topsail by passenger train, make arrangements to get it off afloat." I have also had the job of getting sails on board in an open boat while weather bound under Dungeness and had them sent as far as Hull.

After our overhaul we proceded to Tilbury Dock and loaded a cargo of rice for Great Yarmouth. This rice work was seasonal, the large cargo ships, usually 'City' boats, arriving from the Chinese and Burmese ports between April and July. We had a large contract with Messrs Colman & Sons Ltd of Norwich, the well known makers of starch and mustard. They were now incorporated with Reckitts of Hull. When this rice work was at its height I have seen as many as twenty barges loaded for Yarmouth and Norwich—all Everard's fleet and also outsiders that he had chartered. That was when there was real interest in being a bargeman. We used to sail for turn, that is first arrive, first discharged. The accepted finishing line on these jobs was abreast of Corton Church some four miles to the south of Yarmouth. There were only two tugs available at Yarmouth and they had a busy time towing the barges into harbour when the rice fleet arrived.

In those days there was also keen rivalry between the two tug firms and both tugs would be out of the harbour promptly at 6 am every morning to see which could get a job first. Of late years the Red Funnel Tug Co having sold their only tug the towing has been in the hands of the harbour tug, owned by the Commissioners of the Port. This has not been of any advantage to bargemen for we have had to wait many hours, and even days, out in the roadstead for the tug to condescend to come out and tow us in.

I have sailed into Yarmouth on several occasions and out of the harbour four times but it is tricky entrance under sail and should only be attempted when wind and tide are suitable. The flood tide strikes the south pier and is diverted into the harbour to Brush bend where it shoots over to the nor'ard into what is known as the Sand trap. During the flood an outgoing eddy forms along the length of the north pier and vessels attempting to enter the harbour on the flood tide often get their head in this eddy and go straight for the north pier. With the wind west straight out of the entrance I have found it possible to enter by hugging the south pier on the first of the flood. As my vessel's head clears the pier it is a case of "Down foresail and hard to port on the rudder." The barge then shoots up head to wind in the heart of the tide. Once clear of the entrance it is "Up foresail with the bowline fast on the port side and hard to starboard with the rudder while the vessel is still carrying a little way." If things go according to plan the barge fills off on the port tack at Brush bend and sails up the harbour. I have made as many as six tacks just inside Brush bend with the bowsprit down. Practically sweeping the quay on either side as the barge comes round head to wind. It says much for the handiness of the *Will* when you remember that the average width of the harbour is 300 feet and the *Will* with bowsprit over her nose and rudder is 135 feet long. When the tugs used to come up to Corton Roads or even as far as Lowestoft to tow you into the harbour the towage fee was reasonable. But when, as has been the case of latter years, they charge £6 to pull you through the piers and up the harbour, it is worth a bit of risk to avoid this imposition if possible.

In June 1932 we received an unusual order. We had loaded and were to load many cargoes of refined sugar from Cantly to London, but on this occasion we were to load raw sugar from London to Cantly. Mr Everard had contracted to take the whole consignment of 3000 tons out of an import steamer. The whole fleet of barges had orders to put a new house flag up at the topmast head and proceed to Charlton buoys to load. It is one of Mr Will's little fads that he will forgive many a greater sin, if you are flying a clean house flag. For the rest of the year it was all East Coast work which from October to the New Year meant Cantly to London with sugar cargoes.

1933 proved a disastrous year for me and my reputation was not enhanced. In January we loaded a cargo of coal from Keadby to Margate. When the tug, which had towed us from Keadby to Hull, was cast off there was a strong NE wind. I went chasing down the Humber with the intention of anchoring in Spurn gat. This is an anchorage at the back of Spurn lighthouse and is the finest in the Humber with winds between N through E to SSE. The best berth being abreast of the old lighthouse and about two cables lengths off shore in four fathoms of water. Before I reached Spurn, I thought I could just distinguish a barge's topsail ahead of me. Knowing Jimmy Mole had left Keadby two days previously I assumed it was the *Alf Everard* and kept sailing. There proved to be a dirty sea outside and we had plenty of water on board before we got Cromer abeam to leeward. The wind veered to the east and we could only just fetch the Cockle lightship. We met the ebb tide abreast of Haisborough and the barge was constantly awash. I had gained a little on the craft ahead and could distinguish that it was indeed a barge although it was still hull down. We gained the shelter of Yarmouth roads and had chance for a breather, and also to get some food inside us and dry clothes on. We had met the full force of the ebb tide in the Cockle Gateway and the barge ahead having the smooth water in Yarmouth and Corton roads had gained on us sufficiently to be out of sight.

I found out afterwards that it was indeed the *Alf* and Jimmy later informed me that during the ensuing night the *Alf* pooped herself for the first time since she was new. He was bound to Ipswich and was cutting across the tail of the

Jack Josh/The Everard brothers, Mr Will and Mr Fred

Knocker Hart/Tommy Willis

The Author after being decorated, June 1943

Bawdsey Bank when she did this. The *Will* seemed sluggish and heavy so much so that when I shaped for the Stanford Channel she refused to lift herself up to the seas and just wallowed. I realised there was something wrong and reduced the aft canvas and turned tail. We went back under the lee of the Scroby elbow and anchored in fairly smooth water. I then found the trouble. The *Will* was fitted with six hand pumps, one in the cabin, one the fore side of the aft bulkhead, one on either side amidships, another the aft side of the fore bulkhead and the other in the focsle. Apparently the boxes in the amidships pumps had shrunk. they had been under water nearly continuously for fifteen hours and the barge had a foot of water in her. We had a long, long spell at the pumps but finally drained her. We then jammed the leaking pumps with sacks practically to deck level. Ramming the sacks home with a light stanchion. We then poured six inches of tar over this lot. Unknown to anybody else those pumps remained like this until they were taken out in 1950.

We rode the breeze out for two days when it moderated but still kept from the east. We mustered at 8 am of the third morning and went rolling away for Margate. I kept outside of the Kentish Knock and about 6 pm picked up Margate lights. It was a bit smokey with visibility down to four miles. It was low water and there was still a heavy easterly swell. That meant we had to wait at least five hours before there would be water into Margate harbour; that was if it was going to be fit to attempt to enter. We lowered and furled the jib and topped the bowsprit up. The barge was headed WSW and Margate lights were showing over the port rigging from the man at the wheel. That is where I made my great mistake. I assumed that we were above the Longnose Ledge of chalk rocks which protrude from the cliffs to sea for over half a mile. I also did not allow for the strong tide sweeping to the SSE and the Downs. Before going below for some tea I merely told George the Mate to keep Margate lights over the port rigging and failed to warn him of the southerly set of the tide. George kept the town lights in line with the rigging as directed but failed to notice that to do so the barge's head was steadily veering westward. I had been below for about twenty minutes when there was a violent thump as the rudder struck the ground. I dashed on deck knowing what had happened and told George to heave up on the main brails. We were running with the sails on the starboard side and I wanted the mainsail off to attempt to gybe quickly and get the barge's head off to sea. There were two more heavy thumps and as I pulled the wheel hard to starboard the cast iron steering standard broke and the wheel went forward and down to the deck. With the steering gear smashed the barge took head in and began to pound heavily on the chalk rocks. I was afraid to let go the anchor in case she jumped on it and holed herself, so I just let her keep knocking in towards the cliffs. We stowed all the sails and then stood in the wheelhouse watching the seas curl over the hatches. She continued hammering on the chalk and knocking in towards the cliffs until high water. We then went below for a couple of hours. At 2.30 am the tide had receded leaving us high and dry.

I clambered over the side and made my way in toward the cliffs. I found a roadway and after walking about a mile I came to a garage with all night service. I begged the use of their telephone and rang Mr Will. This was 3 am on a Sunday morning. I gave the required number and presently the operator said "You are through." Here follows an example of Mr Will Everard's alert brain. As soon as the operator said "You are through," I said "Is that Mr Will?" He immediately replied "What is the trouble Uglow and where are you speaking from?" I informed him of my position and he then said "Get back on board, don't allow anyone on board her or assist you. Mr Fred will be down there at 8 am." I obeyed instructions and went back on board.

At 6 am Teddy Parker the coxwain of the Margate lifeboat and two of his crew walked out to us. Teddy was, and is, very genuine and all the while he was coxwain of Margate lifeboat his motto was "Save life first and worry about salvage later." That is more credit than I would give some others on the coast. He said "You are in a bit of a fix old Jim. How did you come to get in here?" I explained and also told him I was not to take assistance. He said "I understand, but I have had more experience of this game than you so here is a bit of advice. Your anchor will heave home through this chalk so what you want to do is run your main anchor out towards deep water as far as you can and then shackle the end of your second anchor cable round the fluke of your main anchor. After doing this take your second anchor out as far as the cable will allow and dig the anchor in. This will keep your main anchor in position." This seemed sound advice and we commenced to follow instructions.

In the middle of our labours the two Mr Everards, Fred and Will, came on board. They asked pertinant questions as to how and why and Mr Will then said "We will send some labourers as soon as possible to lighten her. During the morning get your hatches off all ready." The labourers arrived and we all set to shovelling the cargo over the side. The wind had fined away and the next tide she did not pound so heavily although she would not move. We hove taut on the anchor cable but could not move her. We shovelled coal over the side all that night while shipwrights fitted a quadrant with long arms on to the rudder head. Rope tackles were then attached to the arms and led in board on each quarter to the main horse. We then had a rough and ready means of steering. Altogether we threw 100 tons of coal over the side, much to the joy of the natives who collected round with barrows, prams and even horses and carts.

The following night the *Will* floated and with a light breeze blowing off the land all we had to do was heave the slack of the anchor cables in. The precaution had been taken of running 200 fathoms of two inch wire off to sea and buoying the end ready for our tug to tow us off. This proved unnecessary and we were nearly up to the harbour when the tug picked us up and towed us in. We later had to collect the wire that had been left on the beach and I observed that the *Will* had knocked the chalk boulders perfectly flat for a width of over twenty feet and a length of more than 300 yards when she had come ashore. A motor car could have driven along this causeway quite smoothly.

We discharged the remainder of our cargo and we were then towed to Greenhithe. Once there we were placed on the blocks to survey her bottom. She proved her strength, the only visible damage was a dent about the size of a soup plate under her forefoot. The steering standard was replaced by a mild steel one and we had a general overhaul.

The *Will* was entered as a competitor for the 1933 barge race and with this in view we were fitted with a new suit of sails. Also with a larger pair of leeboards. These, for the uninitiated, consist of planks of wood riveted athwart and held together by steel bars. They are shaped something like a leg of mutton and the narrow end is secured by a steel toggle, through the channel chock, which is connected to a steel bar shackled to the deck. The *Will's* leeboards were six inches thick at the head tapering to three inches at the tail. They were two feet six inches wide at the head seventeen feet long and widening to eight feet at the tail. Barges are flat bottomed craft and when empty, sailing close to the wind, will go sideways like a crab. The purpose of the leeboard is to act as a keel to prevent this sideways movement and hold the barge up to the wind. When in use the tail end is lowered to its fullest extent and protrudes about eight feet below the ship's bottom. When not in use they are hove up alongside on a small hand winch. Our original pair had been made of oak but these new ones were of ash. They were longer, two feet wider across the tail and one inch slighter. When they were fitted I mentioned that I did not think they would prove strong enough. I was informed by those above me that they knew what they were doing.

In February 1933 complete with new sails, the mainsail lashed to the sprit and not over it, we loaded a cargo of oil cake. At this time it was nothing unusual to unload at some channel port and then get orders to proceed empty to the Humber for another cargo. This cargo proved to be for two ports, part for Southampton and the remainder for Newport, Isle of Wight. We discharged the Southampton portion of the cargo first because Newport, IOW is a bad place for water. It required an extra high tide to get 9 feet alongside the quay. We unloaded the rest of the cargo at Newport without undue incident and I was ordered to proceed to Keadby to load coal.

There was a strong east wind and I anchored off Cowes for three days awaiting more favourable circumstances. One morning the wind veered to the SSE and fed up with being at anchor I decided to have a bang at it. Once clear of the Island there proved to be a nasty sea and we made heavy weather of beating up channel. We were standing in towards Brighton on the starboard tack when I observed that the port leeboard was behaving in a peculiar manner. It was secured tightly at the head but instead of lying flush with the barges side was bent in a bow so that halfway down the ship's side it was a foot away from the side. Shortly after it snapped off clean across the chine of the barge. We hove the tail end up on the winch and attempted to come round on the other tack. She refused to wind without the aid of the leeboard so we had to wear her round, stern to wind. Just before we gybed the sails over, the starboard leeboard was lowered. As she gybed this board broke immediately. We do not use the leeboards when the ship is loaded for she then has a sufficient hold on the water without their aid. This was the first testing of the new boards and they proved a washout. We managed to get the broken piece of the port one on board but the other one broke adrift and floated away.

I stood about ten miles off from the land crabsliding all the time. The wind then veered to the SSW and I was able to proceed up channel with a few feet of vang and sheet slacked away. When we rounded the North Foreland and had to pin the sheets in; it was blowing a gale and she heeled over at an alarming angle. It was the first time I had seen her bury her lee rail empty ship. I have said before that the *Everards* were four fine barges but in my opinion should have been a foot wider. They were very tender empty ship. For years I had a fear that the *Will* would catch an unlucky sea when close hauled in a gale and go right over.

We should have been able to fetch up along the Kentish land with the wind SSW but she was going to leeward so badly that we had to make several tacks. I kept the sail on her although at times she was dragging her lee gunwale in the water and showing her weather chine to windward. While punishing her like this the peak of the sail decided to slip down the sprit about three feet and I thought it was going right out of her. I finally sailed her to a standstill at the top of Sea Reach in the River Thames and anchored inside the West Blythe buoy. We had not been at anchor long when I observed one of our small motor tankers passing up river. I hailed the Skipper and told him to tell Mr Will of our predicament. He did so and about six hours later the little MV *Stonebow* towed us to Greenhithe.

I did not get any medals for this trip, Mr Everard suspecting that I had broken the leeboards by catching them on the ground. We had to work all the weekend putting the old leeboards back on and lowering the gear to put the peak of the sail over the sprit end. And even after then I still had to proceed empty to Keadby.

The four *Everards* had been built especially for the Keadby-Margate contract and if there were no cargoes available in London it was a continuous round of coal to Margate and return empty to Keadby. After two Margate freights we loaded three cargoes in succession of sugar from Cantly to Wandsworth Creek, London. This was heartbreaking work. The freightage by the time the extra expenses for towage up and down through the London bridges had been deducted, proved less than a similar cargo for below bridges. The bowsprit had to be unrigged and placed along the starboard deck. Similarly the mizen mast had to be lowered and unstepped to go along the port deck. Everything had to be lowered flat, even the davits being unshipped to allow our passage through the arch over Wandsworth Creek. After passing through the arch and berthing, the main mast, topmast and sprit had to be hove up to allow the cargo to be discharged — then down again for the outward passage. After passing down through the London bridges the barge had to be fully rerigged for the next passage. It was hard, unpaid work.

On 1 June we went on the ways to be spruced up for the barge race. For this event Mr Everard spared no expense. When ready for the race a barge in our firm was rigged as good as new, every shackle and pin, every block and wire, every sail and spar being overhauled and replaced if the least faulty—and very smart the completed vessel looked, with bright varnished spars, freshly dressed sails, white enamelled bow-and quarterboards, the rails in black with the name-badges and sheer streak picked out in gold leaf. the hull was painted with white enamel down to the four foot mark and the lower part picked out in green enamel.

The other three *Everards* had taken part in previous barge races but this was the *Will's* first race. They were too large to stand much chance against the smaller coasters in the confined waters of the Thames and Medway where these races were held, but they made a fine picture and were entered for the races with a sense of sportsmanship more for show than anything (although Jimmy Mole by superb seamanship steered the *Alf* into second place in the 1927 Medway race). The race ended opposite Sun Pier at Chatham that year as it also did in 1928. After 1928 the race started and finished from abreast Gillingham pier. It says much for Jimmy Mole's skill and nerve, that he tacked his huge barge up Chatham Reach both years, among the rest of the thirty competitors without accident or fouling any of the other craft.

For the purpose of racing, the coasting barges were permitted to carry a crew of five and the river class a crew of four. The usual practice with the various firms was to have these crews made up of Skippers in the firm. Some of the Essexmen used to have a local man from the Medway as mainsheetman for the Medway race because very few of them were really acquainted with this river.

Naturally the four big *Everards* were the hardest working vessels to compete in these races, five in crew being only one more than the normal crew and the spinnaker boom, mainsail boom, and the various headsails were all larger and heavier than those carried by the other barges: but it was good fun as well as hard work and we all used to look forward to this annual event.

Messrs F T Everard Limited were generous to the Masters and crews for these events. Apart from any prize money won, which was shared equally by the crew, the firm gave each man £10 for the week's work. For the cup winner—the firm won several—there was a good bonus. The crews of our barges were fitted with white woollen sweaters, white ducks, plimsolls and red stocking caps, all at the firm's expense.

The Thames race used to take priority, the course being from Lower Hope Reach down round the Mouse lightship and back to Gravesend. The day following the Thames race the barges would sail round to the Medway ready to compete in the Medway race the following day.

Our firm used to send on board each of our barges competing, a huge ham, about twelve pounds of roast short rib of beef, a quantity of cheese, butter, bread, milk, tea, sugar and pickles, for the use of the crew. We provided our own beer. There usually was little time to drink it during races and what little we had was soon sweated out of us.

This particular year I was resentful to the fact that Mr Will sent another and older Skipper 'Old Tom Coker', to sail the *Will* in the races. I was nominally the Skipper but still not considered good enough to sail my craft for two days in the river despite the fact that I had been a member of various crews in six previous races. We raced and finished nearer last than first in the Thames and then sailed round to the Medway. There was very keen rivalry shown in these races not only by owners but also by each individual Master and member of the crews. Everard's *Greenhithe* also raced that year skippered for the occasion by Nobby Finch, Master of the *Cambria*.

SAILORMAN

The Medway race proved a remarkable one. There was bad blood between the two Horlocks in the *Redoubtable* and *Phoenician* and once clear of the Medway these two craft sailed five miles to windward of the course because the *Phoenician* would not let the *Redoubtable* pass to windward of him. Nobby in the *Greenhithe* had been over to the north side of the river passing between Port Victoria and the west shore. The *Will* was nearer the south side of the river. Nobby saw that we were going to pass him and edged over to the southward to blanket us and also in an endeavour to put us in the slack tide round Garrison Point. We were overtaking him fast with the wind abeam and the sails on the starboard side. Tom Coker, despite my warning that Nobby would not stand for it, decided to pass to windward of the *Greenhithe*. Nobby reacted as I expected him to, pulled his helm down and luffed up under our lee bow. He was fully entitled to by the rules of the race and it was our place to give way. Whether Tom Coker was taken by surprise or whether he thought Nobby would bear away again, I do not know but he held his course and went head first at the *Greenhithe*. Our bowsprit pierced his mainsail and made a bad tear in it. There was little other damage done because our chain bobstay had just rode upon his rail without breaking and this prevented the two hulls from coming into contact. The two craft took a round turn in the river, locked together, and then drifted apart. The *Greenhithe* was put out of the race and the *Will* although completing the course, was disqualified. I received the discredit connected with this incident from various people who did not know the true circumstances.

Nobby Finch won several cups when Master of the S/B *Cambria*. He was very smart when it came to racing, knowing every trick, legitimate and otherwise, and employing them all. After the usual supper it was all go. "Get round to Greenhithe and put those spare sails ashore and then get away as soon as you can to Cantly."

One little episode which gave me great satisfaction occurred two days before the Thames Race. The *Greenhithe* was also fitted with new ash leeboards but they were only completed while she was fitting out. Nobby took her for a sail to try her out and get everything trimmed to his liking. The first tack he made across the river the port leeboard snapped off as the *Will's* had done previously. The *Greenhithe* returned to the yard and her old leeboards were reslung. I felt that my honour was now vindicated.

I had sailed with Nobby during races as one of his crew and also against him. During one Thames race we were beating up along Shoebury against the wind. For the latter half of the ebb an eddy forms along the edge of the sands, as much as 100 yards wide in places and less in others. It is skill in working this eddy that usually wins races. In the *Cambria* with Nobby at the wheel we were working this eddy close hauled on the port tack. Jimmy Mole in the *Alf Everard* with Tom Coker as mainsheetman was close astern—so close in fact that ten feet of his bowsprit protruded over the top of the *Cambria's* wheelhouse. Nobby knew that when he put about on to the starboard tack the *Alf* would cover and pass him. He said to his crew "When I shout 'Lee Ho!' let your jib sheets fly and then tackle them in the same side when I tell you." He then shouted "Lee Ho!" at the top of his voice and pulled his wheel to port. At the last moment and after he had observed the jibs of the *Alf Everard* flying, he pulled the wheel to starboard. This manoeuvre bluffed the *Alf* off on to the other tack and into the down tide and allowed us to gain a couple of lengths.

Another time, although with a broken leeboard, I saw him keep the *Northdown* covered while tacking through several reaches of the river Medway. Nobby gloried in seeing his crew on the move during these races and would allow very few idle minutes. The *Cambria* had 60 fathoms of three quarter inch cable on deck and if we thought we had time for a sandwich and glass of beer, Nobby would decide he wanted the cable dragged aft. When the next quiet interlude came he would say "I don't think she is doing so well with the cable aft, take it for'ard again." Apart from all this he was a smart man at the game.

Racing over for that year we proceded to Cantly, after more sugar for London, then a cargo of cattle cake to Kings Lynn. The 'Wash Ports'—Lynn, Wisbech and Boston—are not good ports from the point of view of a sailorman. Visibility is usually poor in Lynn Well and the numerous sand banks are steep to. There is a deep with twenty fathoms of water running up the middle of the Well. In hazy weather the hand lead is of little use because the water shoals so abruptly at the edge of the sands. A sailing vessel coming from the south with an offshore wind has to tack up the Well for the coast falls away

SAILORMAN

at Hunstanton in a southerly direction. The present channel to Kings Lynn—between the Ferrier and Bulldog Sands on the port hand and Styleman's Middle and Pandora Sand to starboard—is fairly straight and easy to navigate. This channel, however, has only opened up of recent years. There were many twists in the old channel, the upper end of which is now completely closed. Beating up to Lynn in a sailing barge, if you failed to get up through Lynn Cut by high water, there was nowhere you could anchor without grounding on the ebb. If you failed to get right up it meant turning round and going back for about fifteen miles until the next tide.

The use of a tug is necessary for a sailing craft of any size trading to the Cambridgeshire town of Wisbech. I have sailed up to the docks in the port of Boston but I am not really acquainted with the port. Another small harbour and town to which we carried several cargoes is Wells in Norfolk, a pretty little place with miles of fine white sand for holidaymakers to sun themselves upon during the summer. From a sailorman's point of view it is a different proposition. There is only about nine feet of water at high water springs up to the town; in the winter months the highest tides being between 5 and 7 o'clock, it is dark both morning and evening; the entrance is intricate and the channel constantly altering. There are a few small buoys supposed to be navigational aids but they are not to be relied upon. Those to port entering the harbour are painted black and the starboard hand buoys painted white. These buoys are not moved as frequently as the channel alters. The local pilots know where they lay with regard to the channel but they are the only people that do.

In this connection I once had a good swear off at one of the pilots. We were bound to Wells with a cargo of cattle cake and had been weather bound in Yarmouth Roads with strong northerly winds. Knowing that if I was not in the harbour by the following day I would probably miss my tides and have to wait for another ten days, I banged her down abreast of the harbour. We arrived off the bar at about two hours flood. The wind was blowing straight on shore and the bar was one mass of broken water. I sailed up and down until half an hour to high water awaiting a pilot. As they did not put in an appearance I decided to chance it and take the harbour without assistance. The first buoy in from the bar was on the wrong side of the channel. We struck the ground heavily and

112

although the wind was blowing straight into the harbour the *Will Everard* turned right round twice. While doing this she was knocking in all the time and presently freed herself and we sailed into smooth water. When we reached the safety of the smooth water abreast of the lifeboat house, the pilot boat poked its head round the corner and came to us. The two pilots made the excuse that their motor boat had broken down but I still think that if the *Will* had stopped on the bar, they would have been off quickly enough to render assistance at a fee.

We moored up alongside the quay and stripped the hatchway ready for discharging. The cattle cake we usually loaded was Egyptian cottonseed cake. The cottonseed was pressed into slabs about two feet long by one broad and one inch thick. A number of slabs were packed in a hessian wrapping, which could hardly be called a bag. We used to call this class of cake 'bag cake'. There were what we called ESS greens and ESS reds. The bags with the green stamp averaged about $2\frac{1}{4}$ cwts in weight and the reds were heavier, some weighing over $2\frac{1}{2}$ cwt. I do not think there were a harder working gang of men in the country than the chaps who used to unload us at Wells. The method of discharging was the same as used in most small ports at that time. We would rig up a gin wheel and wire fall on the topsail halliards and topsail sheet. This wire fall was attached to a hand "dolly" winch which was weighted down to the quay by the first four bags of the cargo. One man used to be down the hold and 'snotter' the bags on by the ear, the snotter being a thin chain with a larger link at the end to allow the bight of the chain to pass through. The ear of the bag was the corner where the most surplus hessian was to be found. The cargo was hove out one bag at a time, there being three men working the winch. The bags, after being hove out of the hold, were weighed on a scale placed upon a wooden platform at a height of about five feet. There were four carriers. These four men carried the sixteen and eighteen stone bags on their shoulders; they had about fifty yards to walk and then climb wooden steps to stack the bags in the warehouse.

I was at Newport, IOW in 1951 with a cargo of cattle cake. This type of cake is known as 'Dairy Nuts' and is neatly packed in 1 cwt bags. The method for discharging at Newport used to be as previously described. This last cargo, there were four men in the barge's hold putting rope strops round ten bags at a time. An electric crane was employed to heave the bags up to quay level. Three lorries each with two men on them unslung the bags. When a lorry had two tons on it was driven across to the warehouse a distance of a 100 yards. Here more men unloaded the lorries placing the 1 cwt bags one at a time on a conveyor belt leading to the top of the warehouse. When the bags reached the top of the slack, other men took them from the conveyor belt and stowed them—so much for full employment and progressive tiredness. It is little cause for wonder that costs are high: at Wells we discharged 280 tons in three days by the old method; it took a day and a half to discharge 220 tons by the new.

The pilots at Wells usually joined me in having a drink while we were in harbour but this time I was studiously avoided. After discharging our inward cargo, we loaded English wheat for London. When loaded the wind was still from the NE although moderate. The tides were tacking off so I sent for the pilots telling them that I wanted to get out of the harbour. They said that their fishing boat had not got the power to tow me out with the prevailing wind. After an argument they agreed with bad grace to use two motor fishing boats for towing. The atmosphere was still strained when they cast off outside the bar. I placed several old newspapers and one large Egyptian onion in a paper carrier bag. When the boat containing the two pilots was about a hundred yards away, I shouted and waved the apparently full carrier. They circled and returned to see what I had to give away. Whey they were close enough I tossed the bag in their boat and said "There is something to bring tears to your eyes for leaving me outside the other day."

We always had the problem of getting suitable youngsters to train as crews. For every good lad we shipped we had five who were unsuitable. Sometimes we were three handed, sometimes four. At Wells we shipped a lad of seventeen years of age known as Dick. He was without parents and until coming on board the *Will Everard* had worked on various farms and slept rough. He proved a willing, capable hand and was with us for over two years when he left to better himself. He spoke with a broad Norfolk accent and this led to an incident that amused me. I had been reading the current copy of the Daily Express and in it one of the columnists had written that he spent a hard day on a farm cutting 'Carlic' or 'Charlock'. I said to Dick "You're a farmer's boy, what is 'Carlic'?" He replied "It's something horses hev." Thinking it was some sort of grass, I said "What is it like, is it grass or like a cabbage?" The answer from Dick was "No, it's a pain in the stomick." For his pains he was called a 'dopey Norfolk dumpling'.

CHAPTER 7

My fair share of disasters

1934 passed without any undue incident until November, except for the fact that I found Mr Will Everard increasingly difficult to get on with. While in the *Hibernia* I could do little wrong but for my first few years as Master of the *Will* I could do little that was right. I could never get about fast enough to give satisfaction and began to labour under a sense of grievance. He has mellowed of late but a decade and two decades ago Mr Will was hasty tempered, intolerant of opposition and once he had made up his mind on a subject, would not listen to reason. Early in November we proceeded to Tilbury Dock to load 50 tons of rice and 150 tons of rice meal for Yarmouth. The berth where the rice was to be discharged was not so far up Yarmouth harbour as the berth for the rice meal. I had the rice stowed in the fore hold and the meal in the main hold. After taking in these two parcels I was ordered to the Millwall Dock to load a further 50 tons, this time of gram or dried brown peas. I informed the owner that I would not have sufficient room to take the 50 tons but was told I must take it. By the time we were loaded we had a stack five bags high on the main hatch. I said the vessel was not fit to sail to Yarmouth and was told that I would be towed by one of our steamers. The SS *Audacity* towed me from Greenhithe with a fresh east wind. That night when about a half mile outside the Shipwash lightvessel our towing gear parted. My friendly steamship disappeared into the darkness without making any further attempt to take me in tow.

The wind was blowing straight on the land but as I had a good offing I decided to try and make Yarmouth under canvas. We set the mainsail and foresail and went rolling away to the NNE. She seemed to be behaving fairly well but was very slow so we set the topsail. With all the extra weight above the level of the hatches she was very tender and kept lurching down to leeward. We got nearly to the Stanford channel when she caught an extra puff of wind and rolled to leeward at the same time. The stack of peas was lashed with booms and tackles but the whole lot sagged to leeward. The barge heeled to leeward washing the port sidelight out and then lay at an alarming angle. I pulled the wheel hard to starboard and she managed to come round with her sails on the starboard side. The seas were coming on board one after another. Through the stack shifting, the tarpaulin on the main hatch was torn and she started taking water into the hold. Although it was dark we could see that she was pitching by the head. I ordered the Mate to try the fore pump but this proved to be choked. Fearing that she might go down by the head I sent up rockets and flares off Aldeburgh. This was the first time in my career that I had flared for assistance and my signals remained unanswered.

I wanted Aldeburgh lifeboat to come off and follow me in my attempt to get back to Harwich in case she foundered. I sent up more flares but no lifeboat came off that night. I could see the lights of the town plainly and am sure that my signals could have been seen if there had been an adequate look-out on shore.

Some of the bags of peas were washing about the deck and two had jammed under the main horse: these we cut to pieces with axes. We finally got to Harwich at 9 am next morning. The *Will* had a terrific list to port and was floating two feet by the head. We rowed ashore and I reported my predicament. I was told that the barge *Lady Mary* would be sent to Harwich to lighten my ship. We waited for three days before the *Lady Mary* put in an appearance. We lashed her alongside, rigged a gin wheel up and with the combined efforts of both crews, transferred 60 tons of cargo. This put the *Will* in good trim and we were able to get the water out of her with the aft pumps. Both vessels then proceeded to Yarmouth. When we arrived at Yarmouth I was informed that the 50 tons of rice was to be taken to Norwich. As it was stowed in the fore hold it would have been impossible to steer the barge four feet down by the head. We therefore had the job of carrying 25 tons from

117

forward to aft. As a reward for my efforts on this cargo I had the freightage of the 60 tons transferred to the *Lady Mary* deducted from my money.

If we had a bit of a sticky passage or anything out of the ordinary routine, I would say to Dick, the Third Hand, "What do you think of barging, Dick?" Dick's reply was invariably "Not a lot I don't." At the height of the excitement connected with the previous cargo when I sent up flares I again asked Dick what he thought of it. He expressed his sentiments by saying "I don't think nothin'."

I became so dissatisfied that at the beginning of 1935 I mortgaged my house and with the capital thus raised, invested in a general store. I placed my wife in charge and she ran the business with the aid of my younger brother and a girl we employed. We sold groceries, haberdashery, sweets, tobacco, cigarettes, ice-cream and fruit and vegetables. The business did not show a great deal of profit but it gave me a feeling of independence in case I wanted to 'swallow the anchor'.

During 1935 we did several cargoes to two ports. Freights were scarce and we would load a 100 tons of something in London and make up with fertilizer from Queenborough. This usually also meant two discharging ports and extra expense. We had to chase as hard as possible to make a reasonable living.

Mr Everard had asked me at different times whether my Mate, George Dray, wanted to take charge of a barge. George was married and had also two children. On my advice George had refused these offers because the barges offered were of small tonnage. In 1935 I was asked if I thought George was capable of taking the steel *Greenhithe*. This was a fine coaster of 180 tons burden. I replied "Yes," and George had a jolly good vessel to start with. We had been together for seven years. I got two or three dud Mates after that and it was a year before I got a suitable chap.

In the January of '35 I had a narrow escape from drowning. We were bound light to Cantly from London and had drained down the Thames on the ebb tide in paltry foggy weather. We succeeded in getting as far as Shoeburyness on the first ebb and anchored for the period of the flood tide. At midnight there came a nice little fog breeze from the NW and we hove up the anchor, set the sails and proceeded on our voyage. The night was dark and there was a keen frost. When

An unusual view of the 'Will', 1947

'Glenmore' in the 1953 Thames Match—compare with 1921

The 'Sirdar' racing

the anchor was hove up we discovered that it was foul, the cable having a round turn about the stock. The general procedure in these circumstances to clear the anchor was to make use of the small bowing chain. This small chain was passed round the shank of the anchor and made fast on board. Then about a fathom of the anchor cable was layed over the windlass and out through the hawse pipe. It was usually the Mate's job to stand on the stock of the anchor and pass the bight of the cable round the end of the stock. This cleared the turn from the cable. I stood at the wheel and gave orders for the cable to be cleared. All three of the crew disappeared forward into the darkness to carry out my order. There was neither sign nor sound of them for a quarter of an hour. I grew impatient and hailed the Mate telling him to come aft and catch hold of the wheel while somebody who knew what he was supposed to do cleared the anchor.

He came aft and I went forward. I passed the bowing chain round the shank of the anchor and payed cable over the windlass as previously described. The cable would not run out of the hawse pipe so I stood on the stock of the anchor and with both hands pulled the cable through the hawse pipe. As I did so the bowing chain snapped and both I and the anchor went down with a run. I made a blind despairing grab and managed to find the chain bobstay. My hand rendered down this until it reached the lower end breaking the little finger of my left hand. The anchor had only fallen about five feet under water and I found myself with just my head above water, my left arm extended upwards holding on to the bobstay but my feet still on the stock of the anchor.

The water was icy cold and the barge was going through the water fast enough to press my body against the stem. I heard the deckhand shout in what I thought was a rather gleeful tone "The Skipper's gone." I had the strength to reply "No he hasn't you young B. . . . Tell the Mate to heave to and get this anchor up." They obeyed orders and hove the anchor and myself out of the water. When the anchor was up I clambered on board and went below for a rub down and some dry clothes. I did not discover that my finger was broken until a fortnight later. It was swollen and painful and ached in cold weather so I went to a doctor. He informed me that the finger had been broken and had set badly. He advised having it broken again and reset. I thanked him for his advice but did

SAILORMAN

not relish his ideas. As a consequence I still have a crooked finger.

In February I lost my first spar, a topmast. New rope when it gets wet will fill itself with half-crowns or kinks. We had thrashed up from Yarmouth with a strong SW wind and were about two miles south of Harwich when we broke the topmast. We had rove new rolling vang falls in Yarmouth and these had got wet. As I went about from the starboard to the port tack, the port rolling vang fouled through a kink in the rope in the upper block of the fall. As the sprit came over to starboard the rolling vang still having the weight, pressed against the standing topmast backstay and buckled the crosstree. This left the topmast without any support to windward and it broke at the main mast head and came down with a run. We bore away for Harwich and later anchored to clear up the mess. All the wires and rigging were unshipped from the broken spar, the topsail stowed on deck and the heel of the topmast unshipped. Not to be deterred, as soon as things were ship-shape I had the anchor hove up and we proceeded on our passage.

In August Mr Everard took on a contract to carry cement clinker from Thurrock to Asham, half way between Newhaven and Lewes. There was a cement factory by the riverside and this clinker was discharged directly at the mill. The four big ones were given the job of carrying these cargoes. The contract lasted for two months and we once all arrived at Newhaven together. The only time within my recollection that the four *Everards* were moored in harbour together. We reported to the Agent and then us four Skippers celebrated this unusual event in a proper manner—by that I mean that I had a devil of a hangover next day. Tommy Willis in the *Ethel* was first on turn for towing from Newhaven to Asham and if he felt anything like I did it could not have been a pleasant job.

In October that year we loaded a cargo of barley from London to Beccles. We were too large to go through Oulton Lock at Lowestoft and entered Great Yarmouth. From there we were towed to Beccles: I should imagine that the *Will* is the largest craft that has ever discharged there. We did several of these cargoes throughout the years. It was amusing when towing through the bridge spanning Hadiscoe Cut, to see a butterfly net on a long cane handle thrust out from the shore to the craft towing through. Into this net we dropped the two shillings charged for the bridge.

120

My fair share of disasters

The sea has an irresistable fascination for the true sailor. This fascination is always in his blood and after a few years leaves a man totally unfitted for a life ashore. After a hectic night ashore it is wonderful to be at sea with perhaps the sting of the rain on your face. No temptations, just you and the element that will soothe and caress you in fine weather and challenge and fight you in foul. There is a great peace in standing at the wheel on a fine starry night with only the whisper of the wind for companionship. On such a night the little diver ducks can be heard calling and talking to one another. Or perhaps you are becalmed in early summer and an hour after sunset a little breeze comes stealing off from the shore bringing the sweet scent of May blossom with it. After a few days at home, much as I have looked forward to getting there, I walk in the garden, face the wind and wish I was once more afloat. This feeling is difficult to describe. It is a pain and an urge that is assuaged as soon as you are clear of the land; like the longing for a woman that when satisfied leaves you calm and at peace. I have spent my life since I was first made Master in chasing to get home to my wife and family and as quickly wishing to be away drawn by something that I find difficult to withstand.

After I had bought the general store with some idea of settling down ashore I quickly realised that serving people with $\frac{1}{2}$ lb of tea and 2 ozs of cheese, and so on, was not my forte. Perhaps it was fortunate that I got little time at home because when I assisted in the shop I had not the patience to haggle with old dears as to the price and quality of cabbages. My wife used to say that in six months I would have driven away every customer she had.

In March 1936, my vessel was again in difficulties, this time entirely due to the incompetence of the Mate. We had in a cargo of oil cake consigned to Wells and Kings Lynn. We had sheltered off Great Yarmouth with strong northerly winds combined with snow squalls. About midnight the wind backed into the west and we got under way to go north. We barely saved our ebb tide through the Cockle Gat. I then held her close on the wind and worked her inshore abreast of Winterton Ness to cheat the flood tide. We made little progress and I left the Mate in charge at 4 am while I had a nap, fully clothed, on one of the cabin lockers. Before going below I gave instructions that the barge was to be kept about a quarter of a mile from the land and sailed parallel to it; and, further, that

SAILORMAN

I was to be called if there was any change of wind or the Mate had any doubts. Just before 7 am the Mate came into the cabin and with a cigarette dangling from the corner of his mouth said "We are close inshore and there isn't any wind."

I went on deck and was amazed to see that we were a bare two lengths from the beach and the broken water breaking upon it. I dashed forward, got the bowsprit bobstay up and slacked the anchor off from the bow. I let go the anchor as soon as possible and our stern tailed in toward the shore. The swell was still rolling in from the north and to make matters worse, a little breeze commenced to blow straight on to the land. About half ebb our rudder began to thump on the ground fortunately without breaking the steering gear. Profiting by past experience I unbolted the arms of the steering gear from the rudder and let it jump. Just before low water her stern took the ground and she lay fairly quietly head to wind and sea with the anchor cable leading out to sea.

The Cromer lifeboat appeared on the scene in charge of Coxwain Bloggs. He came alongside the lifeboat first up above the level of the barges rail and then down six feet with the heavy swell rolling in. Coxwain Bloggs said "You are in a nasty position Skipper. How did you come to get here?" I could only say "Ask that useless B. . . standing forward there. He would be doing me a favour if he jumped over the side." The Coxwain tried to persuade me to let the lifeboat tow me off clear as the tide swelled. I knew this meant salvage and refused. I said "I will give you £20 to run my second anchor and 60 fathoms of cable off to sea." He in turn refused to do this. I then said "You don't charge anything for saving life do you?" The reply was "That is our job." I realised that if the vessel was to come off without his assistance an anchor had got to be led far enough to sea to give her chance to sheer from the shore on the flood tide. I said "Right, I am going to lower my boat and we will run our own anchor off: if the boat turns over stand by to pick us up."

Despite the lifeboatmen's remonstrances I had the kedge anchor placed in the boat and one end of a 60 fathom three inch rope made fast on board. The line was then coiled in the boat and the other end made fast to the anchor. We lowered the boat and managed to get the full length of the line led seaward before throwing the anchor over the side. We returned on board and rehoisted the boat in the davits. I had the topsail, mainsail and mizen set and we took the weight on the rope attached to the kedge. As the tide swelled and her stern freed we hove the main anchor cable short. Now came the ticklish part. The rope was led round to the port side and made fast to the fore horse just the fore side of the rigging. As the sails began to fill on the starboard side the main anchor was broken out of the ground. She took the weight on the kedge rope and sheered off a length before coming back head to wind. The main anchor was dropped immediately which prevented her from going head inshore. I requested the lifeboat to let go of me and keep his distance, an unfortunate kick astern on his engines could have put me back in a worse predicament. As she took head off again it was "Up main anchor." This time the flood tide caught her port bow and the kedge rope checking her from the rigging, she began to sail into deeper water. I had the foresail unstowed ready with the bowline to port. As she showed signs of coming back head to wind we hove the foresail up and she continued to check off. As soon as I saw she meant to sail off, I ordered the kedge line to be slipped, steadied my wheel and we were clear. I was thankful to get off with only the loss of a small anchor and 60 fathoms of rope. We managed to get to Kings Lynn without further incident and upon arrival I discharged the Mate.

I have mentioned Cully Toevil as being master of the *George and Eliza* very early in my career. He came to Everards in 1925 and is still with them. He had the *Britisher* for about fourteen years and ever since has been in command of the *Cambria*. Cully, among his friends and acquaintances, has the reputation of doing the minimum number of cargoes in the maximum amount of time. Apart from this his record with regard to damage is practically unequalled. For all the years I have known Cully, I cannot remember him doing any major damage to his ship nor yet to other people's.

He is a tough old boy. About five years ago he had the misfortune to tear one of his thumbs off in a leeboard winch. It pulled clean off with about three inches of tendon attached. Cully was sailing up the Wallet channel at the time and promptly turned round and proceeded back to Harwich. Cully wrapped a rag around his hand and tucked the severed thumb in his pocket. He anchored at Harwich and had a couple of pints before reporting the accident to our agents. In the words of Claude Cann, our agent, "He just walked into the office

SAILORMAN

and said, 'I have had a bit of an accident, is there anywhere that I can get it cleaned up?''' Claude not knowing the nature of the accident said "There is a first-aid station round the corner, I will take you round."
There were two girls in charge of the first-aid post. One of them said "Take that dirty rag off and let me see what is the matter." Cully took the rag off, exhibited his injured hand producing at the same time the thumb. He said "I don't suppose you can put it back on for me?" That was enough for the two girls: one promptly fainted and the other had to sit down. I saw Cully a month later. His hand had healed beautifully. Cully claimed that it was the salt water in his blood that was responsible for this. Asked if it affected him at all, he replied "I have got a bit of a job to hold my pipe but I can still hold a pint." He is a decent old stick who shakes hands with a man because he is pleased to see him and not from force of habit.

In September 1936 I made two fast round trips from London to Wells. We loaded maize meal in London on 1 September '36, proceeded to Wells, discharged and loaded a return cargo of wheat; then cattle cake from London back to Wells and another return cargo of wheat. We were fortunate enough to get out of the harbour on both occasions on the same spring tides which had enabled us to enter. The four cargoes were disposed of in twenty-four days.

It was during this year that my dissatisfaction with conditions came to a head. I handed in a letter of resignation and went home. Mr Will sent for me next day and, determined that I was leaving, I got a lot of things off my chest which would have otherwise remained unsaid. We had two long and stormy interviews which cleared the air on both sides. Since that time I have been a happy and contented Skipper.

In February 1937 I came as near to capsizing the *Will Everard* as I am ever likely to. We had orders on a Saturday afternoon to proceed from Greenhithe to Nicholson's Wharf near London Bridge to load cattle cake for Kings Lynn. It blew hard from the NW so I decided to wait until the day tide on Sunday before proceeding up river. Next morning there was a full gale from the NNW and before going off on board I asked the foreman lighterman if it was imperative that I should proceed that day. The reply was "You must be there for Monday morning's work." There was nothing for it but to have a go. After great exertion we managed to get the anchor up and under way with foresail, mainsail and mizen set. The *Will* made a bad job of tacking up Long Reach. As she came round from one tack to another she would heel over at an alarming angle, skate sideways until she picked herself up and then come up nearly head to wind against her helm. This was because the mizen was pressing her too much. I had the mizen furled, she was then a little easier but very doubtful about winding each time.

We struggled up the river as far as Woolwich and knowing I must not chance her mis-winding in the narrow upper reaches of the Thames, I had the topsail set smart. We were standing up towards the Millwall Dock on the port tack when just above Deptford Creek she caught an abnormal puff. The wind eddies and varies considerably in both direction and strength in amongst the buildings on the riverside. The Third Hand was down the focsle and the Mate was assisting me at the wheel. When this puff of wind hit her she fell straight down on her side. I ordered the Mate to drop the head of the topsail and pulled my wheel hard to port to spill the wind out of her sails.

The Mate foolishly went along the lee deck and was promptly knocked down by a mass of mooring ropes and wires sliding off of the main hatch. I have not a very clear recollection of the sequence of events but remember laying across the top of the wheel, although I was still standing and observing that the top of the 64 foot sprit was about 20 feet from the water. The lee rail was completely underwater and the water was within two inches of the top of the main hatch coaming.

Everything moveable on deck had gone straight over the side even the athwartship battens in the hatchway had slid to leeward until stopped by the rail. I also remember thinking as I watched the sprit and nearing the water "My God, she is still going." I must have staggered forward and dropped the foresail and topsail by the run. My next clear recollection is of paying the anchor cable over the windlass and out of the corner of one eye, seeing the Mate pick himself up from the deck. Our two spare anchors which were stowed in the mast case were lying against the starboard rigging and the focsle companion ladder even had fallen to the floor of the focsle. To judge the angle at which the *Will* had been, the reader must remember that we were only drawing 3 feet of water and that she has 9 feet 9 inches side amidships and the main hatch combings are 30 inches high. There was not another craft in sight underway and the river was deserted.

We had a breather while I got my nerve back and then cleared up the mess and were foolhardy enough to again get underway. The wind seemed to have put all its power and resentment into that particular puff for it moderated considerably during the next hour. We managed to get to the ship from which we were going to load only to find out that our particular consignment would not be working until the Wednesday.

The *Fred Everard* was alongside waiting to load. There was 270 tons of ESS Greens for Wells and 270 tons of ESS Reds for Lynn. Jesse Farthing in the *Fred* was first on turn and decided to take the Wells cargo. It so happened that the stowage was mixed and we got our cargo first. I sailed a day ahead of Jesse. Proceeding down Gravesend Reach the following day with the wind east, Jesse was in collision with a 20 000 ton oil tanker. The tanker was coming up the river against the tide at about fourteen knots and went head first at the port quarter of the *Fred*. If proof was needed of the strength of these four steel barges of Everards, it was given that day. The half inch steel plates were cut through like butter the aft side of the aft bulkhead. She was cut practically to the cabin skylight on deck and the keelplate below, but still kept afloat. The mainsail, topsail and sprit were pulled out of her but nobody was injured. The crew of the *Fred* scrambled into the barge's lifeboat and the *Fred* drifted down the river with her transom underwater. She did not sink however and a tug took her in tow, the crew returned on board and she was taken to Greenhithe. When I returned from Lynn my crew and I had the job of transferring her cargo, which was undamaged, to the *Will Everard*. I thus had two cargoes out of one ship.

That was the end of the *Fred* as a sailing barge. She was stripped and later towed to Fellowes Yard at Yarmouth where she was converted into a fully powered motor ship. Seeing her alongside the *Will* at the present day, very few people realize that they were once sister ships and had sailed some thousands of miles in each other's company.

Previous to these two cargoes we had made a record passage from Great Yarmouth to Dover. We were light on with a cargo of dried beet pulp. We left Yarmouth at 6 pm and were docked at Dover thirteen hours later. My previous best had been in 1935 when George Dray was still Mate. We sailed empty from Yarmouth with a strong NE wind and passed out through Yarmouth piers at 7 am and were moored at Greenhithe eleven hours later: I caught the 6.40 train home from Greenhithe that same evening. On this passage when abreast of the Sunk lightship I observed one of the Harwich-Hook of Holland mailboats coming off. I was running wing and wing: that is, topsail and mainsail squared off on the port side and the mizen squared off on the starboard side. I dare not alter my course for fear of gybing one or more of the sticks out of her. In any case steam is supposed to give way to sail. The Captain of the mail boat who was approaching at right angles to me held his course till the last moment. Possibly thinking it was only a barge and under-estimating our speed, he altered course slightly to pass across our head instead of under the stern. He had to alter course until he was parallel with us and then keep that course for ten minutes before he could get sufficiently far ahead to cross our bows. It must have come as quite a shock to see a sailing barge practically holding him.

In November of that year my old ship the *Hibernia* was wrecked at Runton near Cromer. I loaded a cargo of coal from Keadby to Margate early in the November. When loaded I tacked down the River Humber with the wind moderate from the SE. I saw several barges at anchor in Grimsby inner roads but decided to keep going. We had a long arduous passage, turning every inch of the way. The wind, however, kept light to moderate from the SE and S. The anchor was bowed for eight-four hours, which is a long time for a barge to be underway.

The barges sheltering at Grimsby received the news that I was discharging at Margate and the *Alf Everard* and *Hibernia* came out of the Humber with a freshening northerly wind. Once they were clear of the land the wind increased to a full gale. Jimmy Mole admitted later that it was a dirty old run and he washed his sidelights out.

The *Hibernia* was not too well manned and the Master later said that she sprang a leak and they could not keep the water down with the pumps. He hoisted distress signals and the Cromer lifeboat took the crew off. The *Hibernia* kept going for an hour and a half before she sailed herself ashore and broke up. It was a pity for she was a fine sea ship and I had many a dirty night on board of her. I still think that if a little more nerve and resolution had been displayed, it would have been possible to have sailed her to the shelter of Yarmouth Roads.

We had a good year in 1937 doing twenty-six cargoes on the coast and three river cargoes. The only incident worth recording during that year occurred in the autumn. I had promoted another useless article to Mate. We went in the yard for an overhaul and had the sails repaired and dressed. We sailed from the yard one afternoon and as there were not any orders, I anchored off Greenhithe and went home. That night it blew a gale of wind from the SW and the *Will* began to drag her anchor. Instead of giving her more cable the Mate made an abortive attempt to set the sails and get under way. He tried to set the mainsail and merely succeeded in letting the double sheave hook block on the mainsheet go through the sail two or three times leaving great rents in the canvas. Having done this damage he restowed the sail and with the aid of the other two lads, partly set the topsail. In the meantime the *Will* blew ashore to leeward just above Wouldham cement works. Fortunately it was nearly low water and she grounded on soft mud. The owners phoned me early next morning and informed me of the position of my vessel. I went on board and was in no happy frame of mind when I saw the damage to the newly repaired sails. After dinner, the wind having moderated somewhat and the tide being half flood, we got under way and sailed back to Greenhithe.

I then got orders to proceed to the West India Dock to load. We docked that night and as we were not required alongside the ship to load the next day, a sailmaker was sent from Greenhithe to repair the sails. This meant lowering all the gear again. When the sailmaker had finished the repairs he helped us rig—heave the main mast, topmast, sprit, mainsail and topsail up.

The topmast is hove up on what is known as the heel rope tackle. This consists of a wire led from the heel of the topmast up through a sheave at the main mast head. The wire passes through the sheave and is shackled onto a single block. This block has a purchase led from the deck through the block and back onto the mast case winch. The crew hove the topmast up to within four feet of its final position while I held on the running part of the purchase leading from the winch. The top-mast had a quarter turn in it so I ordered the Mate to take a bar up, place it in the fid hole and turn the topmast so that it would heave right up. This was done and he then climbed to the mast head to prize a topsail hoop clear of the upper cap. He used a ten inch steel marlin spike for this purpose and then—intentionally or otherwise—let is slip out of his hand.

He certainly did not give a shout of warning. I was standing directly beneath, 50 feet below him. The spike hit me on the head, fortunately not point downwards, bounced onto my shoulder and hit the deck. Although nearly unconscious I still held my grip on the wire purchase. If I had let go, the topmast would have come down with a run. I dazedly rubbed my shoulder with one hand and was unaware that I had been hit on the head until the Cook in an awed tone said "There is blood running from under your hat, Skipper." I told him to hold on the wire purchase and then went berserk. With blood streaming down my face I clambered up the rigging with some thought in my mind of throwing the Mate to the deck. Luckily for both of us he eluded me and managing to reach the deck first, ran ashore. I was taken to hospital and had eight stitches put in the crown of my scalp. Thus terminated another Mate's service on the *Will Everard*.

Readers may think that the *Will* has been in more than her share of trouble since I have been Master of her, but I would like them to bear in mind that she has not been 'barging' in the strict sense of the word but thrashed around the coast summer and winter as hard as she could go. I have tamed down now, but for years made it a practice not to turn back until something broke—and sometimes not even then.

The following May the whole fleet, and several outside barges, loaded rice for Yarmouth. There were eighteen all told. I loaded the last cargo of this particular consignment and by the time we were loaded the rest of the fleet had sailed. It was a particular failing of most bargemen that they had the 'herd' mentality. They would wait for each other and gather in a fleet before proceeding. There were strong NE winds prevailing and all the other barges anchored just above Southend Pier. When I sailed I only got about a mile below Chapman Head the first tide before anchoring for the flood tide. The next ebb we went turning away down the river on the principle that you can always come back if necessary. Jimmy Mole in the *Alf* saw us passing and broke away from the fleet and turned away down about a mile astern of us. By the time we had got to the Wallet Spitway the tide was practically finished in our favour. There was a strong wind NNE and a short steep sea. I was pressing everything on the *Will* to keep ahead of Jimmy Mole. We always sailed hard against each other. I even had a small storm staysail set low on the long topmast stay. Abreast of the Spitway we bounced into a sea and the bobstay broke. This is a chain leading from the stem out to the bowsprit end where it is rove through a block and led inboard to be hove taut on the windlass. Its purpose is to counteract the uplift of the weight of wind in the jibs set above the bowsprit. As the bowsprit jerked upwards the weather bowsprit shroud lanyard broke. The bowsprit complete with two jibs jumped right out of its heel socket and went over the side to leeward. We hove to and had three hours hard work getting the jibs and bowsprit back on board. The bowsprit had to be turned completely round for it had been towing alongside heel first.

Jimmy was soon by us and carried on punching down Swin. We managed to reship the bowsprit and rigged a temporary bobstay. This was done by reeving a two inch mooring wire through the bottom link of the broken chain and sinking the whole lot beneath the barge's forefoot. The chain was slacked to its full length and the mooring wire made fast taut on either side to the fore horse. Thus we had a wire led under the bottom of the barge with the chain attached. This was hove taut, a new lanyard rove into the bowsprit shroud fall and we then started sailing her again.

While thus occupied we had lost eight miles of ground previously gained and Jimmy was out of sight ahead. We had Harwich abeam distant three miles by low water the next tide. We kept banging away to the nor'ard, until when abeam of Orfordness the bobstay slipped from beneath her fore foot. The jib was promptly pulled down and commenced to thrash about in the wind. The barge was constantly putting her head under in the sea and it was not fit to send a man out on to the bowsprit to stow the jib. I was supposed to be four-handed but two of the lads were shut down the focsle hopelessly sick and useless. We hove to and I watched her behaviour for three or four minutes. Having but little way on her she did not plunge her head under to each successive wave. I screwed the brake down on the steering wheel and ordered the Mate out on to the bowsprit to stow the jib. I followed him out. He had just reached the outer end of the spar and was standing on top of it when she plunged the bowsprit right under. I was caught about half way along the spar. My feet were washed from the footrope and I hung with my arms clutched round the spar. When she lifted I was so heavy with the weight of water in my clothes that it was as much as I could do to hoist my body across the spar and find the footrope with my feet. However, we stowed the jib and returned inboard, had a rub down and put dry clothes on.

The barge was putting so much water on board that she had to be sailed fine occasionally shaking her up nearly head to wind to enable her to free herself of water. The Mate had no experience of this sort of thing and I stood and steered for the next twelve hours, my only nourishment being a cup of tea and a piece of toast gulped down while steering. Off South-wold, while standing in toward the land, she mis-winded twice, the sea knocking her silly before she was head to wind. Fortunately we were well off when I first tried her and at the third attempt she came about. We towed into Yarmouth harbour at 9.30 on a Friday morning. It had been Wednesday morning when we passed Southend.

As soon as we were moored a gang of men came on board ready for unloading. The firm were anxious for the rice and we were the only barge to arrive. Jimmy Mole had gone into Harwich. It normally took three days to discharge 280 tons of rice with a hand winch. This time, so anxious was the merchant for the cargo, that they rigged two gin blocks up and had two winches. We commenced discharging at 10 am on the Friday and completed discharging at Saturday midday.

My face was caked with salt when we arrived and my eyes were sunken through lack of sleep. After assisting in stripping the hatches, I went below and turned in. Before doing so however, I said to the Cook "I am going to sleep and I am not to be disturbed by anybody, not even if it is Christ himself." Mr Will Everard came to Yarmouth that day about noon. He came to the barge and asked for the Skipper. He was unknown to the Cook who promptly told him "The Skipper gave orders that he wasn't to be disturbed by Jesus Christ, let alone you." The Governor took it very well and merely said "Wake him at three o'clock and tell him Mr Everard wants to see him at Fellowes."

SAILORMAN

I saw him later and he said "I am pleased you got here. There is another full cargo waiting in Tilbury Dock and we have got nothing to put it into. I expect you have had a hard passage, but if you can be at Tilbury for Monday's work, the cargo's yours."

I had a good night's sleep and sailed as soon as we were unloaded. The wind was still from the NE and we were tied up alongside the quay in Tilbury dock before noon on Sunday. We loaded and picked up the rest of the fleet still at anchor off Southend. The wind backed to the west and we beat most of them to Yarmouth on the second round. The firm was having two new ships built at Yarmouth, and both Mr Will and Mr Fred were frequently in the town. Mr Fred had a yarn with several of the Skippers when they arrived and said "You let Uglow do one round you alright." One of the Skippers said in reply "We could all do that if we liked to break gear and blow sails to pieces." He got the reply "Let us do the worrying about losing gear. Uglow did us a good turn and saved us paying landing dues on the other cargo."

After a thorough overhaul in early June, the *Will* once more took part in the barge race. This time I was allowed to sail my own ship and select my own crew. We did not win any cups but with Jimmy Mole as mainsheetman we won the prize for the best seamanship displayed rounding the half way mark. We gybed round the Committee Boat, which was the half way mark that year, clearing her bows by about ten feet. I had intended the distance to be nearer fifty feet but did not allow enough for the flood tide setting past the Committee Boat. No doubt it looked well to the hundreds of passengers and we received quite an ovation. I still possess the fine leather suitcase presented to me at the end of the race.

Racing over, we proceeded to Southampton with a cargo of cement. It is possible to do more cargoes on the east coast under sail than it is to do channel cargoes in an equal period of time, the prevailing winds of the British Isles being westerly. On the east coast the sailorman can use this to his advantage, making passages both north and south with an offshore wind. The channel is a different proposition. During the winter months with a succession of strong SW to W winds it is virtually impossible to get to the westward, sometimes for weeks at a time.

We loaded several of these cargoes for Southampton and in

My fair share of disasters

October the *Will* nearly received her coup de grâce. If a cargo was wanted urgently by the receiving merchant, Mr Will would arrange to have the sailing barge carrying that particular cargo, towed by one of the company's power ships, either motor or steam. Early in October we loaded cement at the Tunnel Works, West Thurrock, and the SS *Glenmary* took us in tow. We were bound to Southampton and there was a strong SW wind. We made heavy weather of it once we opened the South Foreland and had plenty of water on board. Our towing gear consisted of ten fathoms of coir rope, with an eye-splice and thimble each end. Three inch wire was rove through one end by the crew of the ship that was towing us. This wire was bridled from quarter to quarter and made fast. To the other end of the coir spring we shackled our second anchor cable. This was played out as required. We usually had about thirty fathoms out when towing. The weight of this cable used to ease the jerk when in a seaway.

We were about a mile west of the Royal Sovereign lightship when our towing gear parted. Due to the heavy sea. The wind was W by S, strong, blowing at about forty miles an hour. It was the wire bridle made fast to the *Glenmary* that broke and it gave us a decent job getting our cable hove in. I ordered the topsail to be set and we lay full and bye, while all hands hove the cable in and got the towing spring on board. The *Glenmary* circled us and her Master hailed me through a megaphone. He said "Anchor in Eastbourne Roads and when the wind moderates we will take you in tow again."

Captain Brooks of the *Glenmore* had impressed on me in my youth that Eastbourne Roads was not a safe anchorage. I remember him saying "Eastbourne is alright for a fine tide boy, but a ship will not ride if there is any wind." I put aside my doubts thinking we will be out of it in a few hours. I had the foresail set and we proceeded to the roadstead and anchored. We rode on forty fathoms of cable and lay fairly quiet. The *Glenmary* steamed around for about two hours without anchoring and then to my surprise proceeded to the westward. We had not sufficient manpower on board to heave the anchor up and our only recourse was to ride it out.

That night the wind backed to the SW and increased to a gale. We rigged and let go a second anchor and spent an uncomfortable night. The following day the wind backed to the SSW without moderating. I then found the reason for Captain

Brooks' warning. Although anchored half a mile from the shore, the rebound of the sea on the land and the undertow, made the *Will* continuously first ease up on her cable and then set back with a jerk. There was a terrific strain on both cables and windlass. I made a rolling hitch with the end of thirty fathoms of five inch manilla rope around the forty five fathom shackle on the main cable. This spring was then led through the fairlead and back to the main mast. I then eased about ten fathoms of cable out and rigged another spring from the foreside of the windlass. This spring was made fast to the cable and also taken back round the main mast. Both ropes were then secured to the mast and the remaining five fathoms of cable payed out. This arrangement somewhat eased the jerk on the cable and the weight on the windlass.

Towards dusk of the second day the wind increased to hurricane force: it registered ninety miles an hour on the shore. I ordered the focsle hatch to be closed and locked and a canvas cover was placed over it and wedged in place. I followed the two members of the crew down the cabin and we had some tea. I warned the lads that we would probably have to get out of her that night and gave them life-jackets. I also took the precaution of putting the ship's papers and one or two valuables in a small leather grip. The barge was rolling and jerking so badly that it was practically impossible to stand on deck. There was so much water coming over her that the waves were occasionally breaking over the top of the cabin hatchway. I put on my oilskin coat and placed a packet of twenty cigarettes and two boxes of matches in one of the pockets. I jammed a dry towel on top of this and went on deck to watch from the wheelhouse.

The lights of Eastbourne were continually being obscured in the blinding rain squalls and the wind was howling through the rigging in one continuous roar. At 10 pm the motion became easier and her head banged away towards the shore. With a shout of "She has parted her cables," I roused the crew onto the deck. I nipped below, grabbed a tin of red flares and my grip and returned to the deck; the cabin hatch was closed and secured; and I sent up six flares in rapid succession to let those on shore know we were coming in. I then ordered the crew into the rigging and followed close behind them.

Going aloft was no picnic and we had to hold on tooth and nail against the pressure of the wind and the violent jerking of

Seven cups from seven races—the Author's trophies

The 'Will' racing

The 'Sara' in the 1953 Thames race—note the foresail boomed out below the spinnaker

'Sara's' crew after the 1953 Thames Match

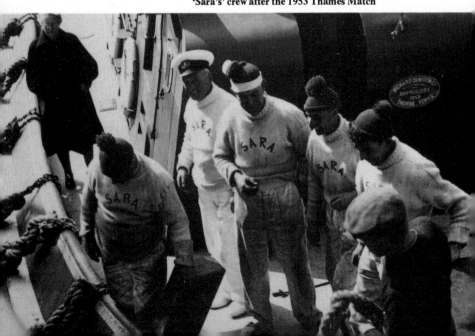

the rigging as the mast rolled in its case. I guided the lad up the rigging keeping my arms about him so that he would not be jerked over the side. He whimpered and asked me if we were going to drown. Much against my better judgement I cheerfully told him there was nothing to worry about. The Mate reached the level of the crosstrees and sat on the cross-tree bed plate holding on to various wires with both hands. The lad and I stood on one of the wooden battens lashed athwart the narrow upper rigging. I secured a topsail gasket around us and waited for her to hit. It seemed as if the old *Will* knew it was a matter of life or death for as we approached the broken water and the combers peeling up on the beach, I observed a huge concrete groin ahead. I knew it would be curtains for her if she hit it and so did she. By some miracle she took head off and passed clear. She also passed the only two remaining groins to the eastward of her before paying away head in. Then with a violent jar she struck, lifted herself and struck again. I saw the ship's lifeboat picked up bodily out of the davits by a sea and flung against the main mast. The boat broke in half and the next sea took it out over the bow. The sickening pounding continued for an hour and then as the tide ebbed and she made a bed for herself, quietened and merely stirred uneasily as an extra huge sea hit her. I asked the lads if they would like a smoke and withdrew the towel from my coat pocket. As I did so a huge wave hit her and my pockets were filled with water from the spray that came mast head high. We did not have a smoke.

By midnight the decks could occasionally be seen free from water. Half an hour later we saw the flickering light of two electric torches approaching. They came to a stop abreast of us and the beams of light were directed first aloft and then down to deck level. By their light I could make out that the *Will* had knocked a wall of shingle up level with her rail along the port side. I shouted to let the persons holding the torches know that we were aloft. A faintly heard voice was heard to shout "I think you can get ashore." We watched our chance and as she freed herself temporarily of water, jumped for the deck and then ashore. It afterwards transpired that the crew of the Eastbourne lifeboat were still making unsuccessful efforts to launch their boat four hours after we went ashore.

Our escort of two men guided us up the beach and led us to a small bungalow. There we were given a thorough rub down and dry clothes by the good people of the house, and hot tea laced with brandy. We were then led to a summer chalet with a tin roof which was however equipped with two comfortable beds. I spent the rest of the night listening to the wind making desperate but unavailing efforts to lift the roof off. I pondered whether I could have got sufficient canvas on the *Will* to have kept her off and run back up channel. I comforted myself with the thought that no canvas would have withstood the fury of the wind and that the wind was so far on the land that she would not have worked off in any case.

At daybreak next morning I roused the lads out and we returned to the beach and were able to clamber on board. I took stock of the damage and we set about getting things squared up. The sea had forced the wedges out of the hatch battens on the starboard side of the main hatch and a certain amount of water had penetrated the hold. The tarpaulins were rebattened in the coamings and new wedges driven in. The jib had washed from its gaskets on the bowsprit and had to be restowed and lashed more securely. The broken cables were hove clear of the windlass and various ropes hauled on board, coiled up and relashed.

The tide was now coming in and although the wind had moderated, the seas would soon be breaking over her again. We therefore went ashore and had breakfast. I was then driven in a car to the nearest telephone and informed Mr Will of the sequence of events. The owners by now had complete faith in my judgement and I was merely asked what gear I required sent down to enable me to refloat my vessel. I asked for anchors and cables, a 100 fathoms of two inch wire, a new boat and the temporary steering quadrant that had been used once previously, to be sent; also for a shipwright to rig the quadrant and two labourers to assist with the anchors. The steering gear had been hopelessly smashed and so I also asked for new steering gear to be got ready. The men and gear arrived in the afternoon but there was little we could do before daylight next morning. The tides were neaping and next day the water only reached four feet up the *Will's* side at high tide We hired a horse to drag the boat down onto the beach and also the anchors and cables. One anchor was stowed on board and the other led along the beach close to the low water mark. The cable was then hove taut. The steering quadrant and tackles were rigged and there was little more that we could do.

My fair share of disasters

I kept the owners informed of the position and was told that
the SS *Glenmary* was being sent in to Newhaven to await my
instructions for a suitable opportunity to tow us off. Four days
later with the wind touching off the land, the *Will* refloated
herself. I put the labourers ashore and sent a message for the
SS *Glenmary* to come immediately. We set some sail, hove the
anchor up and sailed into deeper water. When the *Glenmary*
appeared on the scene we passed her one end of the 100
fathoms of wire and told her to take the weight of the tow. The
Master of the *Glenmary* had but little experience of this class
of work and promptly parted the tow wire. We then reverted
to our old method of spring and cable and told him to take the
weight gently. At last we got the anchor up and headed for
Newhaven.

There was still a heavy sea and with the quadrant and tackles
we had great difficulty in steering the *Will*. I could see we
would soon be adrift again and this time probably finish up
under Beachy Head. I signalled to the *Glenmary* to reduce
speed to slow and to let a barrel of oil drip over his stern to
stop the seas breaking. He did this and the oil had a magical
effect, taking the tops right off the seas. We finally moored in
Newhaven harbour before dark. The *Glenmary* proceeded on
its way and we had a further three days being fitted with new
steering gear. The first thing I had done after refloating was
have all the pumps sounded but even after the awful pounding
she had received the good old *Will* had not made any water.
We later proceeded to Southampton without further assistance.

Rumours of war were already in the air and after passing The
Nab and Spithead I observed that a boom defence was being
built across the Solent as a precaution against submarine attack.

A week or two later poor old George in the *Greenhithe* was in
trouble. He had in a cargo of oil cake for Wells and dragged
ashore in Yarmouth Roads during a SE gale. The *Greenhithe*
was later refloated and towed into Yarmouth, where her cargo
was discharged and stacked in a warehouse. The *Greenhithe*
then went into dry dock and had eight new plates put in her
bottom. The cargo was reloaded and George made another attempt to get to Wells. He got as far as Cromer and caught in
another gale of wind, blew all the sails out of her. He accepted
the assistance of the MV *Lowestoft Trader* and was towed

back to Yarmouth. The cargo was again discharged and despatched to Wells by rail. From the time the *Greenhithe* first loaded to the cargo being discharged for the second time was eleven weeks. Partly due to the strain and worry and partly to the weakness left on his chest when he had pneumonia in the *Hibernia,* George cracked up and was seriously ill for nearly three months.

It was a bad winter for barges. We were in another breeze at the latter end of November when several barges were tempted out of Yarmouth by the official weather report. I received the report over the wireless at 7.55 am while sailing down the Solent; we were bound empty to London after discharging another cargo of cement. The forecast for the Isle of Wight, Dover and Thames areas was: winds variable or westerly, light. Within six hours there was a violent gale SSW in the Channel and S in the southern North Sea.

Of the Yarmouth fleet, the *Northdown*, Master A Roberts, was the only barge that succeeded in getting as far as Harwich. She received such a caning that she jarred one of her pumps through her bottom. Of the others, the *Una* was beached at Corton and the *Royalty* was assisted into Yarmouth. Three of Goldsmith's barges were abandoned: two of these fetched the Dutch coast and the third was picked up off the coast of Germany.

The *Will* ran up the Channel under jib and topsail sheet like a scalded cat. She is normally an easy steering ship but that day, between Dungeness and the South Foreland, it took three of us to steer her. The seas were so steep that as she tipped on top of a sea her rudder came clean out of the water. The helm had to be corrected smartly so that when the rudder again met the water, she did not yaw. I believe if she had been allowed to broach to, she would have turned over. As it was she shot a hundredweight drum of red oxide from an inner cupboard in the wheelhouse. The drum cleared the eighteen inch step in the lavatory and smacked up against the rail. It was the only time I saw the *Will* poop herself when empty. I was pleased to get the partial shelter of the Downs off Deal. We went close inshore to the north of Deal Pier and anchored.

For every passage like this there were fifty ordinary ones that are not worth recording. The sea-going bargeman looks forward to the all too short summer to get a breather before the autumn gales commence.

My fair share of disasters

1939 proved a good trouble-free year for the *Will Everard*. We loaded and discharged our cargoes with the regularity of clockwork and we were not involved in any breeze worth mentioning.

The country was preparing for the inevitable war and the Naval Control system for the routeing and protection of merchant vessels was established in August. We loaded a cargo of cement for Southampton on 28 August. I had to go to the Naval Control office for instructions. This was on the Thursday before war was declared. The officer who supervised my clearance was either a prophet or had more knowledge than the general public. He merely said "Hurry up and get there before the balloon goes up on Sunday." On the strength of this information I temporarily evacuated my wife and children to the Midlands. Before sailing I was called into the boardroom by Mr Will who enquired if there was anything I needed for the ship in view of the impending war. I asked for and obtained a new set of code flags and jokingly said "Do you supply poor bargemen with binoculars?" He replied "Stop at Greenhithe and I will give you a pair."

I had previously asked Mr Fred whether the firm would make an indoor steel shelter of my own design from old ships' plates. They had not only made it but sent men to my home to bolt it together in the position it was to occupy in my dining room for five years. I asked Mr Fred how much I owed for this shelter and he replied "Pay us after the war." That bill is still outstanding.

I anchored off Greenhithe that evening and Mr Will gave me a pair of binoculars that had belonged to his father, with the words "Take care of them Jimmy, they were the old Dad's." Knowing the sentimental regard all the members of the family had for their father's memory, I was very surprised at this gesture. Taken in conjunction with the air raid shelter, I decided that even shipowners were human and worth studying a little more.

We arrived at Southampton in time to hear Mr Neville Chamberlain's announcement that we were at war. When the *Will* was once more unloaded, my orders were to proceed back to London. Southampton being a big ship port the Naval Control did things in a big way with a huge block of offices at their disposal. I had to go there for my clearance and was interested to see so many gold braided figures poring over maps and

SAILORMAN

charts. One old RN Captain came over and after studying my papers said "Ah!—this is interesting, a sailing vessel bound to London." Another old boy came up and with his mind on anti-submarine action, said "Can your vessel zigzag Captain?" I solemnly assured him that my deckhand could zigzag with the best when left at the wheel and further that if the wind was from the east the *Will* would zigzag all the way up channel. He seemed satisfied and I was allowed to proceed. In 1938 the firm decided to convert the *Alf Everard* into a power ship. Jimmy Mole, after a temporary period as Master of the boomie *Martinet* took charge of the MV *Signality*. At the time this was written he was still Master of her but has always regretted the circumstances that forced him out of his *Alf Everard*.

Early in 1938 a new Master, Bob Roberts, joined the firm. He took over the boomie *Martinet* from Bobstay Bill, a man who had become mentally ill. Roberts had had a chequered career in schooners and about four years as Mate and Master in spritsail barges. I believe, with a companion, he had at one time sailed a small fishing boat to the West Indies. In the 1950s, upon the retirement of Cully, he took over the *Cambria* and later when sailing the *Cambria* independantly of Everards, he achieved some fame—due to publicity on the BBC—as 'the last of the sailormen.' I never knew if he bought the *Cambria* from Everards, but do recall Mr Fred once telling me of one of his father's sayings, which was "If you have a grudge against anybody sell them an old sailing barge," implying that the upkeep would cost more than the returns.

140

CHAPTER **8**

Barging in wartime

The first little bit of excitement we had in connection with the war occurred about a month later. We were on passage to Norwich with a cargo of wheat and about two miles ENE from Southwold. The wind was NE and I had been tacking to the nor'ard keeping well off the land. I was below getting some dinner when there was a violent concussion as if we had gone head first at another ship. I dashed on deck and asked the Mate what he had hit. As I spoke I saw a destroyer tearing along about a quarter of a mile outside of us. A column of water rose well clear of his stern and there was another underwater exposion. I realised he was laying a pattern of depth charges and probably flushing a submarine and I did not wait for more but promptly bore away for the shore. We hedge hopped the last fifteen miles making short tacks along the land.

The next trip in company with the barge *Britisher*, we sailed for Yarmouth laden with rice. We were abreast of Southend at 3.30 pm with a fresh SW wind and the weather was dirty with rain. I had intended anchoring at Yantlet for the night but as the *Britisher* kept going, I chased after him. It was dark by the time we cleared the Nore and I shaped for the Middle Barrow lightship. I soon found out that all light buoys and the lights on the lightships were extinguished. Failing to pick up the Middle Barrow and doubtful of my position, I sounded continuously with the lead: I had lost sight of the *Britisher*. The water shallowed to four fathoms and I swung the barge head to wind and ordered the anchor to be dropped. This was done and the sails stowed. The wind increased to a gale and riding on a short scope, fifteen fathoms, the cable parted at about 3 am. We scrambled the sails on and spent an uncomfortable four hours tacking from side to side of the Barrow Deep, waiting for daylight and with only the hand lead to guide us in our sounding.

At daybreak I found I was indeed in the Barrow Channel and turned and ran for the Swin. When it got nicely daylight, I saw the *Britisher* running through the Black Deep, an unbuoyed channel three miles outside of me. Harry Delaney her Skipper evidently saw the *Will* at the same time and shaped in for my stern. By the grace of God he came across the top of the Sunk Sand without grounding. We arrived at Yarmouth before dark without further incident.

The Admiralty now established a rule that small craft, which included barges, were to anchor between the hours of sunset and sunrise. What my Lords of the Admiralty did not realise was that you cannot anchor with impunity in the North Sea—not in a barge at least. It is easy enough to let go the anchor but the weather can deteriorate a lot in fourteen hours during the winter months. The *Will Everard's* main anchor at this time weighed just under 10 cwts and normally it was never let go in more than seven fathoms because in more water than this it was physically impossible for the small crew to heave it up. Trying to follow the instructions with regard to anchoring at sunset, I lost four anchors during the war years.

During the following five months we loaded several cargoes of rice from London to Norwich consigned to Messrs Colman Ltd, now Reckitt and Colman. This rice was stored and later the store received a direct hit with a bomb, caught fire and the contents were destroyed. So our efforts for five months literally went up in smoke. An order had been issued compelling all small sea-going craft to carry a wireless receiving set so that Masters could keep up to date in case of instructions being given in an emergency. In early March 1940 I again loaded cement from London to Southampton. By then the enemy had started dropping magnetic mines. The Navy had already found the answer to this menace but very few merchant ships had been degauzed or wiped by an electric shock passed through the vessel to alter the magnetic pole.

When I received my routeing instructions from the NCSO in London I found that I could proceed through the overland passage to the North Foreland. That is through the Four Fathom and Gore channels. From the Longnose buoy the route was to a position one cable's length from the North Goodwin lightship and thence along the inner edge of the Goodwin Sand on a given route one cable (100 fathoms) wide. This route was five miles further to sea than I would normally have proceeded. For a start I kept strictly to instructions and on the first day (a Wednesday) I anchored off Yantlet at the mouth of the Thames just before sunset. At daybreak next morning there was a strong wind ENE and it wanted two hours to high water. I decided that if I could tack along the Kentish land and get off to the North Goodwin, I could then bear away with a fair wind down Channel. We made a good lead on the port tack and fetched Whitstable Street buoy before standing off the land.

By the time we had worked down to the North Foreland there was a nasty sea caused by a combination of a strong head wind and an outgoing tide, and once clear of the Foreland, the *Will* commenced dipping her head under and picking up green water. I could see a large naval craft (an examination ship) anchored near the North Goodwin lightship and also several merchant ships of about 2000 tons. I also observed a couple of large aeroplanes, fitted with some circular arrangement from nose to wing tips and tail, sweeping to and fro about fifty feet from the wave tops: I later found that this was an experiment to set off magnetic mines.

When I had got to a point half a mile from the position where I hoped to bear away and run with the wind and sea on my port quarter, a large tug steamed towards me. When it got within hailing distance a voice shouted through a megaphone "Let go your anchor." We had got as much sea as we wanted and fifteen fathoms of water. I replied "If I let go my anchor in this amount of water the crew will never be able to heave it us again." Again came the order "Let go your anchor immediately." Determined not to lose another anchor within a period of six months, I decided to fox the person who was giving these unwelcome orders. I stressed the obvious and shouted "This is a sailing vessel, it will take time to get the canvas off of her." I then ordered the crew to stow the mizen to let them see that I was trying to obey orders. At the same time I bore away a couple of points and eased a couple of feet of vang and main sheet off. This was just as the *Will* liked it and she started going through the water at about eight knots. It was as much as the tug could do to keep up with us. I then gave the order "Heave up on your main brails and half stow the mainsail, but take your time." There was a final hail from the tug. by this time we were two miles from the position where I had originally been hailed. Suddenly the tug turned and steamed back. I bore away and the *Will* ran to the Little Downs, to the north of Deal, like a scalded cat.

Whilst disliking the thought of losing a fair wind and anchoring on a lee shore, I did get the sails stowed and anchored in six fathoms of water. We rode uncomfortably with forty fathoms of cable out for sixty hours. Nobody came near us and by Sunday Morning I was nearly frantic in my desire to get on with my passage. The wind had fallen light and backed to the NW and I knew that I had lost the chance of a fast run down Channel. About 10 am I picked up the binoculars for the thousandth time and scanned the shore and the fleet of ships anchored about five miles to the NE of me. I observed that they were moving and had just passed a sultry remark to my Mate to the effect that every other blank was allowed to proceed but us, when there were two violent explosions and two of the ships settled and sank. I found out later that they were Norwegians and that the authorities knew that the Jerries had dropped magnetic mines in the area. That was the reason for anchoring and also for the aeroplanes I had seen. I—in my cleverness—had sailed right over the top of them three days previously.

Ten minutes later a launch came off from Deal and a naval officer shouted "You had better get away from here Captain: it is an uncomfortable corner of England." Without telling him what I thought about the people in charge of that particular corner, I immediately gave the order to heave up the anchor and set sail. I sailed all night and next day, went through the farce of taking a Trinity House pilot from the Nab to Southampton waters, and then a river pilot up the River Itchen. This was due to more foolish instructions that all vessels were to come under compulsory pilotage. The pilot was a nice enough chap who had been used to piloting the big liners in. He admitted that he knew nothing about barges and was quite content to supply me with cigarettes whilst I proceeded as if he was not on board.

We discharged our cargo of cement and then loaded a cargo of South African sugar from one of the Union Castle ships, for London. I again received instructions to keep to a restricted route up through the Downs for the voyage back to London. The sight of the two ships being blown up the week previously had impressed me considerably. After having fetched up channel with the wind from the north, it veered to the NE when we were abreast of Dover. I knew that I would not be able to tack up through the Downs to the North Foreland in the restricted route given to me and yet was eager to get up through and carry a fair wind to London. I decided to take the chance and told my crew that I would give them a £5 bonus each if we were round the Foreland before dark. I consoled myself with the thought that if I was alive to pay the bonus, it would be worth it and if not I would not have to pay. They got their bonus and I had completed a fast passage.

After this cargo, because things were getting a bit sticky with the mines, I was confined to the River Thames taking cargoes of cement from the Tunnel Cement Works at West Thurrock to ships in the various London docks. We were in the Millwall Dock discharging when the Dunkirk evacuation began. The Government wanted volunteers and were commandeering all the barges and small craft they could to assist in the evacuation. The *Will Everard* was not at Dunkirk for the sole reason that the dockers refused to finish completing the discharge of her cargo during their dinner hour. The barges that were going to Dunkirk had to be assembled down stream that afternoon and we were not in a position to catch the tide out of the dock. I volunteered to take the place of 'Dick the Dagger'—Captain Miller—of the barge *Royalty*. He was then a man of sixty-five years of age. I was told to stop on my own ship and Dick took the *Royalty* over. The *Will Everard's* sister ship, the *Ethel Everard,* Captain Tommy Willis and the *Royalty* were both lost at Dunkirk. Old Dick was awarded the BEM for his part in this epic.

In June 1940, the *Will* was again laden with cement bound to Southampton, but this time she was towed by the SS *Agility* Captain J Bennett. As we passed Dover in the dark hours, the French coast was ablaze with fires from Dunkirk to Boulogne. During the previous twenty-four hours there had been an order issued that no merchant ship was to proceed inside a line from the Owers lightship to St Catherines Point in the hours of darkness. Neither Captain Bennett nor myself were aware of this and we proceeded in from the Owers towards the Nab Tower in the first false dawn. When abreast of the Nab, there was a bang and a shell whistled across the bows of the SS *Agility*. The Master ordered his engines to be stopped and we observed an MTB approaching at speed.

I would like to digress at this point to say that at this period many decent young chaps with a little yachting experience and various city types with a bit of pull had been given temporary commissions in the RNR. They learned fast and did an excellent job, but in the first eighteen months of the war there were many clashes between these young officers and the old salts of the Merchant Navy. Captain Bennett was a phlegmatic type when at sea and it took a lot to ruffle him. As the MTB drew near we observed a young officer on the bridge clothed in a peaked cap and vivid striped pyjamas, and with a megaphone to his mouth. After asking the names of our two ships, cargoes and destination, he ordered us to proceed back to the Owers until sunrise. This may have been fair enough but he added that gauche remark "Don't you know there is a war on?" Bennett, who was leaning on his port bridge rail, removed his pipe from his mouth, picked up a megaphone and shouted "You won't win it in your . . . . . . pyjamas, will you."

By the time this cargo had been discharged, the Jerries had established their big guns on the cliffs opposite Dover and had commenced firing at ships passing through the Straits. In view of this I was informed that I was not allowed to proceed up Channel to London. Mr Everard asked me to see if I could find any local work in the Solent and told me that for his part he might be able to get me a few cargoes of cement from Medina Mills, to Southampton or Poole.

The Government had now placed restrictions on all small craft under a certain length and not commercially employed with power and ordered others to be rendered useless in case of falling into enemy hands in a possible invasion. This placed me in a rather invidious position. The cement mill was situated half way between Cowes and Newport, IOW. The distance between points at East and West Cowes is only about 150 feet and as there were no tugs or motor boats to give me any assistance, I had to do my best to navigate the *Will* under canvas. In addition I was forbidden to sail between sunset and sunrise. As I was still sailing by the share I looked like being in for a lean time and I could also see prospects of doing considerable damage.

I did a couple of cargoes of cement from Medina to South-ampton and then managed to get several cargoes of coal from Southampton to Cowes. I was not very popular with the locals because there were several small Thames barges owned in this area that had been working between the Island and the mainland for many years. Their average cargo was about 100 tons and they did not like the idea of the *Will* scooping the pool with 300 tons of cargo at a time.

I had my first experience of bombing in August. We had loaded coal at Phoenix Wharf on the River Itchen and were sailing down this narrow river under full canvas bound to Cowes. It was a fairly heavy daylight raid and the weather overcast with rain. We could hear the drone of many planes and an Ack Ack battery at Shirley opened up. We were just approaching the end of Southampton Docks when we heard the scream of falling bombs. At this stage of the war the Germans had a device fitted to the bombs which caused them to make a very frightening noise—something like a screech owl in a fit. As soon as we heard the falling bombs the crew jumped down the focsle and I left the wheel and disappeared down the cabin just as fast. After the first moment of panic, I realised that my ship was running down river under full canvas with nobody on deck. I returned to the deck and grabbed the wheel, the bombs had already landed on the shore and one of them had evidently found a target where there was some small arms ammunition stored. There was a huge plume of smoke and various minor explosions. I slacked the sheets right off and could not get away from Southampton fast enough.

The next cargo I had a brush with the RNVR. We had discharged cement at Poole in Dorset and I went to see the NCSO at Poole for routeing instructions. He cleared me and told me which signal flags I was to fly. He also informed me that if I could give him a definite time for passing Hurst Point, I would be allowed to proceed through the North Passage into the Western Solent. The Needles channel was closed to shipping and failing this I would have to go right round the Island and come in from the Nab. There was a westerly gale blowing and I said that I would pass Hurst Point at 4 pm: this I did. The *Will* was squared right off with main-sail and topsail to starboard and the mizen gybed to port. We were going through the water, empty barge, at 9 knots and with the aid of a spring tide were passing over the ground at between 13 and 14 knots. When nearly abreast of Yarmouth, IOW, a fast launch attempted to close us from the shore. I observed a young officer in the bows and a sailor armed with a rifle. As soon as he was within hailing distance, this young hero shouted *"Will Everard,* stop, you are flying incorrect flags."* I shouted that it was a sailing vessel and that it was impossible to stop. I saw him consult the sailor and he then shouted "heave to." This was a more seamanlike order and I rattled her to head to wind and with great difficulty got the sails sheeted home and the foresail aback. We were still soaking sideways at 5 knots with the flood tide when he gave the order which made me consign him to hell and give voice to my opinion of landlubbers in uniform. The order was "Come ahead and maintain your position." After a swearing match on my part he said "You may proceed as far as Cowes and I will see that you are not allowed out of the Solent. I will also report your language and insolence." Whether he had the power to do this I do not know but it is a fact that I had to be content with local cargoes for the rest of 1940.

It is difficult for the ordinary landsman to appreciate the hazards and difficulties of sailing a barge round the coast or the physical and mental strain imposed on the men who manned these craft during the war. According to regulations and orders, they were restricted to inshore routes where all light buoys and lighthouses were extinguished; all the lightships were withdrawn after the enemy aircraft had shot up one or two and even some of the unlit navigation buoys were taken up or deliberately placed on the wrong side of fairways with the intention of deceiving the enemy. The barges were supposed to be at anchor from sunset to sunrise and only proceed during the hours of daylight; but, as I have said, the Admiralty did not realise that you cannot always anchor in the North Sea with impunity especially on a winter's night with half a gale of wind blowing on the land, not in a loaded barge with a foot freeboard and only a hand windlass to get the anchor up again.

A sailing barge working to windward in a moderate breeze will make about 3 knots on a fixed course into the eye of the wind. In other words, assuming that the direction one desires to go is north and the wind is north, a barge would be three miles further to the north at the end of an hour. If there is a three knot tide against her, the net gain at the end of six hours sailing would be nil. During the winter months with only eight hours daylight, it sometimes happened that the tide would be against the barge for six hours which only left two hours out of twenty-four to get ahead. No weather reports were allowed to be broadcast or printed and the bargemen had to rely entirely on their own judgement with regard to the weather. Naturally it was impossible for these craft to sail in convoy nor yet detail craft off for their protection. Their only means of defence against enemy aircraft or a possible E-boat was one 1917 pattern Ross rifle to each craft. Yet despite these conditions barges carried valuable food cargoes round the coast during the war with some degree of regularity. This was no mean help in the war effort.

Some idea of the hazards run can be gained from the following true narrative.

In November 1941 the *Will Everard* had discharged a cargo of rice at Norwich and in company with the barge *Britisher* loaded a cargo of empty wooden cases for London. The two vessels stopped at Great Yarmouth for two days awaiting suitable weather and then sailed for London. Before sailing the Master of each vessel had to report to the NCSO who gave him routeing instructions as far as Harwich. They would not give routeing instructions direct to London in case enemy aircraft laid magnetic mines during the time the craft were on passage from Yarmouth to Harwich. By the time the two Masters, Harry Delany and myself, had obtained permission to leave the port and engaged a tug to pull us out of the harbour, it was 11 am.

There was a light breeze off shore from the NW but due to the delay, by the time we were clear of the harbour, the tide had set against us. We both made slow progress and by sunset were only about two miles above Southwold. The wind had now freshened from the NNW and the flood tide was just drawing with us. Under normal circumstances the two craft would have been at Harwich within the next six hours but naval orders were orders and that meant anchor at sunset—5 pm. The two craft were anchored but by 9 pm the wind had veered ENE and was blowing half a gale of wind to the land. A nasty sea also got us. As Master of the *Will,* I tried riding on fifteen fathoms of cable knowing that if I gave her more, myself and crew would not have sufficient strength to heave it in and get the anchor at sunrise.

The sea increased and at midnight, due to the short scope of chain, the anchor cable parted. It was a black night and not a glimmer of light was visible anywhere to distinguish the coastline from the sea. The *Will* had the unenviable task of running in the direction of Harwich and the treacherous sands of the Thames Estuary. I knew that if I was seen the vessel would probably be fired on by the shore batteries or by some naval patrol craft. I decided that it was best not to attract attention, as at this period of the war gunners were likely to fire first and ask questions afterward, so ran without navigation lights and completely blacked out.

I had to keep sufficient way upon the vessel to make a true course and yet hold her back as much as possible waiting for daylight to navigate the intricate channels between the sand banks. I hoped that if I could find my way into Hollesly Bay, the water would be smoother and perhaps I could hold her until daylight with the small second anchor. With this end in view the second anchor was rigged and shackled to the cable. Unfortunately it had a collapsible stock which was pushed through the crown of the anchor and secured with a key pin. This was done and the anchor lifted over the side. The vessel was bouncing in the sea and the anchor kept banging up against the stem of the vessel. It could not be seen at the time in the darkness but this continuous banging knocked the key pin out of the stock and the stock disappeared from the anchor rendering the anchor useless.

I put the Mate at the wheel and sounded my way along with the constant use of the hand lead. I was sufficiently acquainted with this part of the coast to sound my way along the inner edge of the Sizewell Bank and then ordered the Mate to steer a course which I estimated would take us half a mile clear of Orfordness: we were running over the tide with only the topsail set. At 4 am the water shoaled from ten to two and a half fathoms, and I knew by this that I was clear of Orfordness but doubtful if we were passing over the northern end of the Whiting Bank or the middle of the Bawdesy Bank. Knowing the tide was easing against me, I had the topsail lowered then bore away SW and ran under bare poles knowing that the *Will* would be past Harwich before daylight unless she stuck on one of the sands.

By now I also knew that I had no means of anchoring my

'Sara' and 'Veronica' laid up at Greenhithe, 1963

Greenhithe, 1963. The end of the 'Dreadnought'—literally

vessel. The defence boom at Harwich was closed during dark hours so I could not take the chance of running in and beaching her. I had no wish to send up distress signals and risk having a salvage claim made against me so decided that if I could keep afloat I would make direct for the Thames. Half an hour later I passed within a hundred yards of a blacked out destroyer with my heart in my mouth—but I was neither challenged nor fired upon. At 6 am we passed three trawlers anchored in line and estimated that they were anchored below the Cork lightship. The water shoaled to two fathoms and I knew that I was crossing the flats off Harwich and approaching the Naze. At 7 am it was break of day and I was able to distinguish the Naze abeam and get a true position.

Then I had my next worry: we had to sail up the Wallet Channel and out through the Wallet Spitway. This could not be classed as a channel as it only carried three feet of water through at low water and sometimes even dried out. I had often given a wry grin when reading my routeing instructions, for this particular stretch of water: "Barges will proceed keeping at least six feet of water under their keels." It was the only route allowed at the time to barges and when we were loaded down to her plimsoll, we only had three feet of water under our bottom at high water.

I had previously had uncomfortable thoughts of coming into contact with a magnetic mine at this point, not passing over one. I knew that with my present draught I could not get through the Spitway until half flood so I had to set all plain sail and heave to waiting for water over. I had no knowledge of how the *Britisher* had fared but at 9.30 am saw her approaching rapidly with all sail crowded on. The wind was now ESE fresh and at 10 am the *Britisher*, which was drawing a foot less water, passed me and sailed out through the Spitway. Poor old Harry, little did either of us know that when he passed and hailed me in the Wallet Channel, it would be the last words I was to hear from him. As he passed me, he gave a wave and cheerfully shouted "Any minute now." He left a widow and three fine children.

I waited for another quarter of an hour and then followed the *Britisher* out. Once clear I set all sail so that I could get as far up the Thames as possible before the tide came against me. Knowing that with the wind blowing up the river and the tide down, I could control the *Will* and moor her to a mooring buoy without assistance. At 11 am we had passed the Maplin Spit buoy and were rapidly overhauling the *Britisher*. Although worn out by lack of sleep and worry, once clear of the Spitway I allowed the two crew to lay down and was now on deck alone. I stood on the weather side of the wheel and was using the *Britisher*, which was running leewardly as a steering mark over my starboard mizen shrouds. The *Britisher* was about a quarter of a mile ahead and a similar distance to leeward toward the Maplin Sand, when suddenly where her sails had been was a thick oil black column of smoke 300 feet high. Before hearing the explosion I knew the *Britisher* had detonated a magnetic mine; then came the roar of the explosion and the *Will* shuddered as if she had come into head on collision with a dock wall. Small pieces of debris pattered on the hatches and decks from aloft. The crew tumbled on deck looking startled. "The *Britisher* is gone," I said simply; "Stow your mizen and pick up half your mainsail."

As has been narrated I had been unable to go into Harwich for further instructions and assumed that several mines had been dropped during the night. I bore away and sailed for the spot where the *Britisher* had disappeared. My stomach muscles tightened as I awaited another explosion which would be death. I picked up my binoculars and scanned the water. There was nothing, only small pieces of matchwood. The *Britisher* had been a wooden vessel and had been blow to smithereens. I said to the crew "Keep your eyes open, there might be a chance." But it was hopeless. After five minutes of peering I said "Alright, set your sail again, let us get up as far as we can God willing." We met the ebb tide at 4 pm at the bottom of Gravesend reach. I kept sailing until my vessel was barely making headway and at 5 pm succeeded in mooring to a buoy just above Tilbury Coaling Jetty. The sails were stowed and I went below, washed, changed and had the crew put me ashore.

My home was at Gravesend and after I had crossed the ferry from Tilbury, I went into a phone box and telephoned the owners. I contacted the foreman lighterman and informed him of the loss of the *Britisher* and her crew. He said "You go straight to the Naval Control and let them know the position and the time." My reply was "I'll do nothing of the sort, I have been on my feet thirty-eight hours and I have had enough." Mr Will then came on the phone and said "Alright

Jimmy, we will let them know, you get a night's sleep and see me at 10 in the morning. Don't worry about your ship, we will tow her up the river without you." I went home and instead of sleeping, lay awake for hours wondering if, and hoping that, my eyes and ears had deceived me at 11 that morning.

Subsequently Mr Will fought hard and established a precedent by obtaining a Royal Naval Lieutenant's Pension for the widow and children.

The war continued and we had our share of scrapes including being hunted by German E-Boats of Harwich in 1942. On the night of 3 March 1943 I was at home and in bed with my wife when the air raid sirens sounded. The battery of Ack Ack guns at Denton had already opened up so it was a belated warning. We tumbled out of bed and hustled the children downstairs to put them in the indoor shelter afore-mentioned. There were three loud explosions in quick succession, a hell of a clatter and all the lights went out. My wife was flung against the stair case by the force of the blast and although she never complained at the time, injured her spine and is still suffering from the after affects to this day. Three bombs dropped in our short road. The first demolished three houses and badly damaged many others. We had all the slates blown from the roof, windows blown out and some structural damage. Next morning when the damage could be seen, we found a fifteen foot ornamental tree had been uprooted on the other side of the road and was firmly planted upright on the roof of my house. A neighbour dryly remarked that the enemy pilot must have known I was a keen gardener.

I stayed at home until 7 March whilst temporary repairs were effected and then proceeded to Ipswich where a cargo of cement had been discharged from the *Will*. My orders were to proceed to London for another cargo of cement. The cement was urgently needed for building runways on new airfields for our air force. On the morning of 9 March 1943, we were running up along the edge of the Maplin with a nice NE breeze. We were squared off, with good visibility and the sun just rising, when I observed about eight planes flying low, coming off the land from the direction of the River Blackwater. I did not claim to be an expert on aircraft and assumed it was some of the lads off on a dawn raid. It afterwards transpired that they were enemy fighter-bombers which had raided a factory near Ilford used for the manufacture of ball bearings. The

153

SAILORMAN

Mate and Third Hand were in the wheelhouse and the Cook was just stepping out of the focsle hatch. I walked to the main horse with the intention of taking a look under the mainsail for a view to leeward. Suddenly there was the roar of a plane's engines and within seconds the sails were riddled with bullet holes. I heard the rattle of hailstones on the deck and by the time I had decided that they were bullets, a black aeroplane with white crosses clearly displayed passed straight over us about 100 feet above the topmast. The bow plates of the *Will* were pitted with indentations. One cannon shell had passed through the galley funnel forward within a foot of the Cook and two had pierced the steel low down on the starboard side of the wheelhouse. By some miracle nobody was injured and as the Jerry had a Spitfire on his tail, he did not come back for another go. When telling the story later I claimed that I beat him by sheer speed. He was doing about 250 miles an hour and I claimed that by the time I dived head first into the wheelhouse, I was doing 300.

Later in London I had to fill in a long questionnaire in triplicate answering such questions as time, place, type of air-craft and so on. When I came to the question "Was the air-craft hostile?" I put "Very." We had to have a new suit of sails. In early May I received a letter stamped OHMS and marked *Secret and Confidential*. When I opened it, I found that it was from the Lord Chancellor's Office and the contents informed me that I had been awarded the MBE, but that the matter was confidential until it appeared in the Honours List. I later received another letter telling me to attend an In-vestiture on 25 June at Buckingham Palace, where I would be decorated by the King. I informed Mr Will and he congratulated me. I said "I have never worn uniform in my life, if I go up there in a decent double breasted blue suit it should be OK." He replied "You will do nothing of the sort, you have been awarded the decoration as a Captain in the Merchant Navy, you will dress accordingly. Go to my tailor and ask to be fitted in my name." I did so and after choosing the best material, was duly measured.

On the 25th, I presented myself at the Palace. I had been given two tickets for relatives to watch the ceremony. I took my wife and elder son. The wife's mother was staying with us and insisted on coming to London as well. I pointed out that she would not be admitted but she said "I don't mind, I will wait outside of the gates." My wife and son were ushered into a large room where about another hundred proud relations were already seated. There was a dais mounted in the front like a stage and a hidden orchestra was playing quietly. I was ushered into an ante-room where, with others of all the armed forces, I was lined up in order of precedence and an usher gave us the drill—mount the dais, face the King, salute and stand to attention whilst the citation is read out and he puts your decoration on; then, step back three paces, salute, turn right and walk away. Despite the solemnity of the occasion, when it came to my turn, to mount the dais, to my amazement I saw Gran sitting in the front row with a beaming smile on her face. It later transpired that she had wandered by the guards at the gates of the Palace into the courtyard. She was a tiny little person and when a policeman accosted and questioned her, she said "My son is in there being decorated and I haven't been given a ticket." He said "I will see if I can wangle you in, Mother." He succeeded and she said "I really do think you London policemen are wonderful." The proudest moment of my life followed when the late King George the Sixth pinned on my decoration, congratulated me and shook hands. My impression at the time was of a very handsome man and—a curious thing to say about a man—the most beautiful blue eyes I have ever seen.

One thing marred my pleasure: two months later I was presented with the bill for my uniform. I disputed it telling Mr Will that it was his idea and he ought to pay for it. He said it would look bad if it was known that the firm had had to pay for the uniform of one of their Masters and he was sure that a man in my position and with my earnings would not wish for it. I paid the bill and after taking the gold braid off and substituting black buttons, it made a fine going ashore suit for several years.

During the war years the *Will Everard* carried more than 42 000 tons of cargo, grain, sugar and cement from port to port, mostly on the east coast. Her only crew consisted of the Master, Mate and a lad; her only armament was a Hotchkiss gun and a rifle. However there have been a surfeit of war books and many thousands of civilians in the towns and cities of south and east England had equally harrowing experiences as I have mentioned.

CHAPTER 9

Post war
-the end of an era

Now on to the post-war years: by 1950 there were only about six barges trading north of Yarmouth or west of Dover, the *Will Everard* and *Cambria* and the rest owned by the Rochester Trading Company. The spirit of competition was dead and I no longer had the pleasure nor incentive to try to beat the other man or men. I had always been impatient of delay and after a year or more of seeing other barges go by me, with the assistance of an engine, I finally persuaded Mr Will to put an engine into the *Will Everard*. By October 1950 the conversion was completed and the *Will* was given a new register. I do not know if there are more ship's registers like it but the *Will* was described as 'The Motor Sailing Ship *Will Everard*'.

Whilst the *Will* was being converted, the two brothers Mr Fred and Mr Will did not always see eye to eye with regard to the details. Between them they gave me some awkward moments. During the conversion an entirely new cabin had been built for the Master over the engine room and it had earlier been decided to french polish it. About two weeks before we were ready Mr Will and Mr Fred made their usual 9 am visit to the *Will*. This particular morning Mr Will said "I don't think we will french polish that cabin, Jimmy, but we'll give it two coats of good varnish." Mr Fred promptly said "Do you know of a good french polisher at Gravesend Jimmy?" I replied a Mr Arbin made a good job of repolishing a bedroom suite when we were bombed. He then said "Get him up here and tell him to polish that cabin."

When it had originally been decided to convert the *Will*, Mr Will said to me "When she comes off I want her rigged exactly the same as she is now." About three months later Mr Fred, with whom I never had a mis-word in thirty two years service and who treated me as if he were a benevolent uncle, said "You won't need a bowsprit with the engine will you Jimmy?" "It will be a nuisance in the docks," I replied, so he said "Right, we will take the wooden collar boards off, put steel ones on, finish it off with a fish plate and make a neat job of it." Just before we were ready Mr Will asked if everything was alright and I said "I am ready but the fitters have got another weeks work." He said "What do you mean you are ready? Where is your bowsprit?" To this, I explained, "All the bow rails have been altered and the bowsprit bitts burnt off. It will mean putting new bitts in and burning a gap in the starboard collar board." He then said "I don't care what it means. I told you she was to be rigged the same. Fit a bowsprit out."

Half an hour later Mr Fred appeared and I told him what his brother was insisting on. With a twinkle in his eye he said "Rig something up that looks like a bowsprit and when you get to sea throw it over the side." I had a double right angle piece of steel bolted on to the central pawl bitt for the windlass, to take the heel bolt of the bowsprit and a carved hollowed-out chock bolted onto the fish plate. This was to grip the bowsprit when it was down and it then rested on top of the rail, just clear of the starboard snatch. I then selected the *Sara's* old racing bowsprit which was lighter, slighter and easier to handle than her original heavy spar. This was completed and three days later 'Old Jock' the painter was cutting in the name *Will Everard* with gold leaf. Mr Fred was watching him and, possibly hoping for a bit of praise, Jock asked "Is it alright sir?" Mr Fred said "Yes, but while you are at it put some on the end of the bowsprit so that Mr Will can see it." I was pleased to get to sea two days later.

Mr Will's insistence that despite the engine the *Will* should remain fully rigged, later proved a mistake; with her top hamper she would not make headway if the wind exceeded Force four Beaufort scale. If it was Force five or over she would not even look at it and had to be tacked as if under sail alone. I also made a mistake in ever asking for the engine because the extra money earned did not pay for the smell and the dirt and the fact that I was often tempted into going to sea with an unreliable engine, when normally I would have kept in harbour. When having the engine installed it had been my intention to use it to save towage into and out of harbour, dock work, and to use it when becalmed or in light airs. However, when she was ready Mr Will considered her as a fully powered motorship and expected me to make passages in any weather, which lead to a situation where I was resentful and he thought I was falling down on the job.

In 1953 it was decided to resume the Thames and Medway barge matches, the last previous ones being in 1938. I had sailed either as crew member or Master in the previous matches 1927 to 1938 with the exception of 1929 when the death of the founder of the firm, Mr F T Everard, caused the firm's entries to be cancelled. In 1953 Mr Will asked me if I would skipper the *Sara*. I said I would be proud to, on condition that I could pick my own crew from the ships in the firm, to which he agreed. In all previous races the *Sara* had been skippered and manned by Mistly men employed for the occasion. This had been a sore point with me and other Skippers in the firm because it inferred their superiority as bargemen. That year was Coronation Cup year and the two matches were condensed into one. The combined Thames and Medway Coronation Barge Match.

Possibly by a fluke the *Sara* won handsomely. There was a cup for the Master of the first barge over the line, one for seamanship and one for winning. I am very proud to say I collected all three cups. Conditions were not ideal, light variable winds for the down passage which later turned to moderate WSW for the beat back. I was fortunate enough to drain over the starting line first, with a sneaking air from the SE—I had previously listened to the weather forecast which said "light southerly winds". After the start the wind dropped altogether for an hour and most of the barges drifted in the heart of the tide over towards Thameshaven. I managed to hug the south shore along the edge of the Blyth Sand and picked up a little southerly draught that only extended about fifty yards from the edge of the sand.

Because of the conditions the course was shortened and the committee boat, the *Royal Sovereign* was anchored about a mile below Southend Pier and used as a rounding mark. We had established a two mile lead when this happened which was shortened to a mile by the time I had run to leeward across the river to round the committee boat. The wind freshened from the SW but we still had a comfortable lead at the bottom of Lower Hope Reach although Gill's *Sirdar* seemed to be overhauling us a little. After having quite a tussle to pass the *Glenmore,* the barge that I had first ran away to sea in thirty-three years before, the *Glenmore* broke her topmast at the top of Sea Reach and that put her out of the running.

My crew seemed to think the race was won although I warned them that we had got to race to the finishing line. When racing, it is the practice after tacking to make the lee jib sheet fast rather slackly and it is the jib sheet man's job to control the flow of the sail with the aid of a handy billy tackle snottered to the rail and the bight of the sheet. Jack Nunn (later to sail the *Veronica* to victory in subsequent matches) was lee jib sheet man. He was sitting on the weather rail holding a fair tension on the tackle whilst swopping jokes with the other jib man. He was not paying sufficient attention to his job and as he rocked backwards laughing, the *Sara* caught a head to wind puff and Jack went overboard. He held on to the end of the tackle and was being towed at about 6 knots abreast of the fore horse with the jib pinned in the fore stay. I had to shake the *Sara* up head to wind three times before he was finally hauled on board. We lost a lot of ground but still won the race. For his carelessness and ultimate recovery I was awarded the Seamanship Cup.

Although I am afraid some of the opposing Skippers considered the whole affair rigged, I again skippered the *Sara* in both 1954 matches—once more separate races on different days—and was fortunate enough to win both. Mr Gill, owner of the *Sirdar* was a thorough sportsman and at the annual dinner after the Medway race, told Mr Will Everard that he would continue to spend money and try until he beat *Sara*.

In November 1954 the strain of being 'Top Skipper' proved too much for me and after suffering from a slipped disc in the neck, phlebitis, neuritis and general strain, I had to come ashore. My doctor, who had always been interested in my career, wrote a letter to Mr Will in which he said that if I was not taken out of the barge, he would hold Mr Will personally responsible. I had been a sailorman for thirty four years and obstinately refused to take a real motor ship. The Governor was good enough to give me a staff job in charge of the firm's oil installation and wharf. I was unsettled and like a fish out of water: I did my best to cope but possibly the owners expected more from me than I was capable of in this particular field.

In 1955 I was temporarily released from my shore duties to fit out and sail the *Sara* once more. That year the *Sirdar* appeared with a magnificent new suit of sails, her hull polished and gleaming and also sporting a new type of leeboard, copied from the Dutch: this had the head set six inches out from the rigging chock and five inch wide runners set on the sides of her hull from abreast the fore to just abaft midship, so that when the leeboard was down there was no dead water between the board and hull. The combination did the trick and despite two close races, the *Sirdar* skippered by old Tom Cooke, deservedly won both races with *Sara* second. After the races I told Mr Will that in my opinion in future, in a true run race, the *Sirdar* would beat *Sara* nine times out of ten. Despite his disappointment, he said "Right, we will build something to beat her."

The *Veronica*—another famous old racing barge—had been allowed to deteriorate and her hull had lain on the foreshore at Greenhithe for about five years. Mr Will had her stripped and re-built, one timber at a time and one plank at a time, until she was entirely rebuilt to her original lines. When she was ready Mr Will asked me which I wanted to sail and I replied that, on principle, I could not desert *Sara*. He then said "Who shall we put in her" and my immediate reply was "Jack Nunn. He was her Skipper for a few years, knows her and has had as much experience of barge racing as I have."

In the 1956 Thames Race I made a false start in *Sara* entirely due to the fault of the committee. Our orders distinctly said that at 10.50 precisely a warning gun will be fired for the river staysail class; at 10.55 another gun will be fired, this gun being for the staysail class to start and a warning gun for the river bowsprit class; at 11 am precisely a gun will be fired for the river bowsprit class to start. Due to the committee boat coming late on station they decided to postpone the start of this class by five minutes. The committee boat, which was to be the starting post was anchored on the south shore above Lower Hope Point. I had been jilling over the north side of the river and heard the first gun go off. I had an excellent watch and just before 10.55 said "Keep your eyes and ears open for the second gun." When my watch read 10.55 one of the crew said "I saw a puff of smoke." We then prepared to race. I timed it beautifully, with topsail and mainsail squared off on the port side and spinnaker on the starboard side and a nice SW breeze.

We approached the starting line. When 50 yards from the line Mr Will, who was on the committee shouted "There is another gun, Jimmy." I am afraid that in front of a thousand spectators I went haywire. I shouted back ". . . the gun, time is time." However we were recalled and by the time we had got back to the line, we had lost a lot of ground. The result of both the Thames and Medway races that year was *Veronica* first, *Sirdar* second, and *Sara* third.

In 1957, whether it was due to my outburst the previous year or because they had spent a lot of money on my unsuccessful ideas I do not know, but Mr Will tactfully informed me that in future, my job being so important, I could not be spared for barge racing. Ironically enough, it was my old friend Jimmy Mole who had left the firm in 1951 and I had got back to go mainsheetman with me in 1953, who superseded me.

To be fair, for the 1956 races, Mr Will had given me carte blanche to put all my ideas and theories into practice. For a start, I had a high sheeted foresail, designed like, and tended as a jib. I also decided on a high peaked mainsail with a short head rope. It was as near to Bermuda rig as you could get in a sailing barge. The *Sara* proved to be slower than she was with her square gear. It seems that the designers of sails in the latter part of the last century and the beginning of this, knew their job, with regard to sails for this particular type of hull. All old photos and paintings depict them with very square mainsails even in some cases with an overhanging peak. On the other hand the shape of the leeboards I suggested was accepted and they were used in both *Veronica* and *Sara* until they finished their sailing careers. I still think that the high sheeted foresail would have proved a success but Mr Fred, who was on the committee boat, did not like the look of it and as soon as the Thames race was over had it altered into the normal sail in readiness for the Medway Race.

In April 1958 I had a final set to with Mr Will and left the firm. Many years before in one of our periodical rows he had said to me "Look here Jimmy, we are of a similar temperament and both have tempers but you have got to remember, I am your employer." He asked me to rescind my decision but I had had enough. Mr Will died in June 1958.

SAILORMAN

In September 1958 my wife and I became tenants of a local public house The Brown Bear. Ninety per cent of our customers were seamen of all nations, and with my intimate knowledge of their particular breed, and of ships, and also my wife's motherly interest and forbearance of their adjectives, the place became quite famous. It became known to seamen all over the world: at Christmas we would get cards from places that practically encircled the globe. Although the pub has now been pulled down, to this day on a cliff overlooking a quiet Norwegian fiord, a large arrow is painted and the words *Brown Bear 600 Miles,* a relic from some thirsty seamen. We retired in December 1970 and still enjoy an active life as Senior Citizens.

POST SCRIPT

Readers may be curious as to the ultimate fate of some of these racing craft. After the Centenary Matches of 1963 and the death of the second Mr Fred Everard, the younger generation of directors decided to break up the *Sara* and *Dreadnought.* We do not know the pressures that caused them to come to this decision. A contributory cause no doubt, was the high cost of maintaining three first class yachts to be sailed on only two days in the year. The late Mr Will and Mr Fred had been very conservative in their outlook on the barges and had kept up the tradition and, in some things, the methods of their own father. The third and youngest generation have completely modernised the firm and have a different outlook. Also they may possibly have felt that by selling them, they would give offence to some of the unlucky would-be buyers.

In 1965 they did finally dispose of the hull of the *Veronica* to a private buyer, I believe, on the condition that she was never to sail again. In 1967 they finally disposed of the *Will.* Thus ended an era. She was sold to the owner of a yacht barge at Malden and after changing hands once more is now completely re-rigged as a sailorman by some enthusiast. She is now fifty years old and I will guarantee that no other sailorman has ever had as much salt water over her as the *Will.* Mr Maurice Gill's *Sirdar* was left without practical competition and he no doubt felt that enough was enough. As I look back, our generation may not have been as well off financially but we were of necessity tougher and more resilient. *Sweat* was not a dirty word, to be covered up by perfume but the result of honest work. I wish I could see the return of the community spirit and togetherness shown by the British people in the period from 1940 to 1945. When faced with all the complex difficulties of modern times and conditions, it would be as well if people would remember the motto of Navvy Brooks: "There is no such word as cannot."